HALO
THE MASTER CHIEF COLLECTION

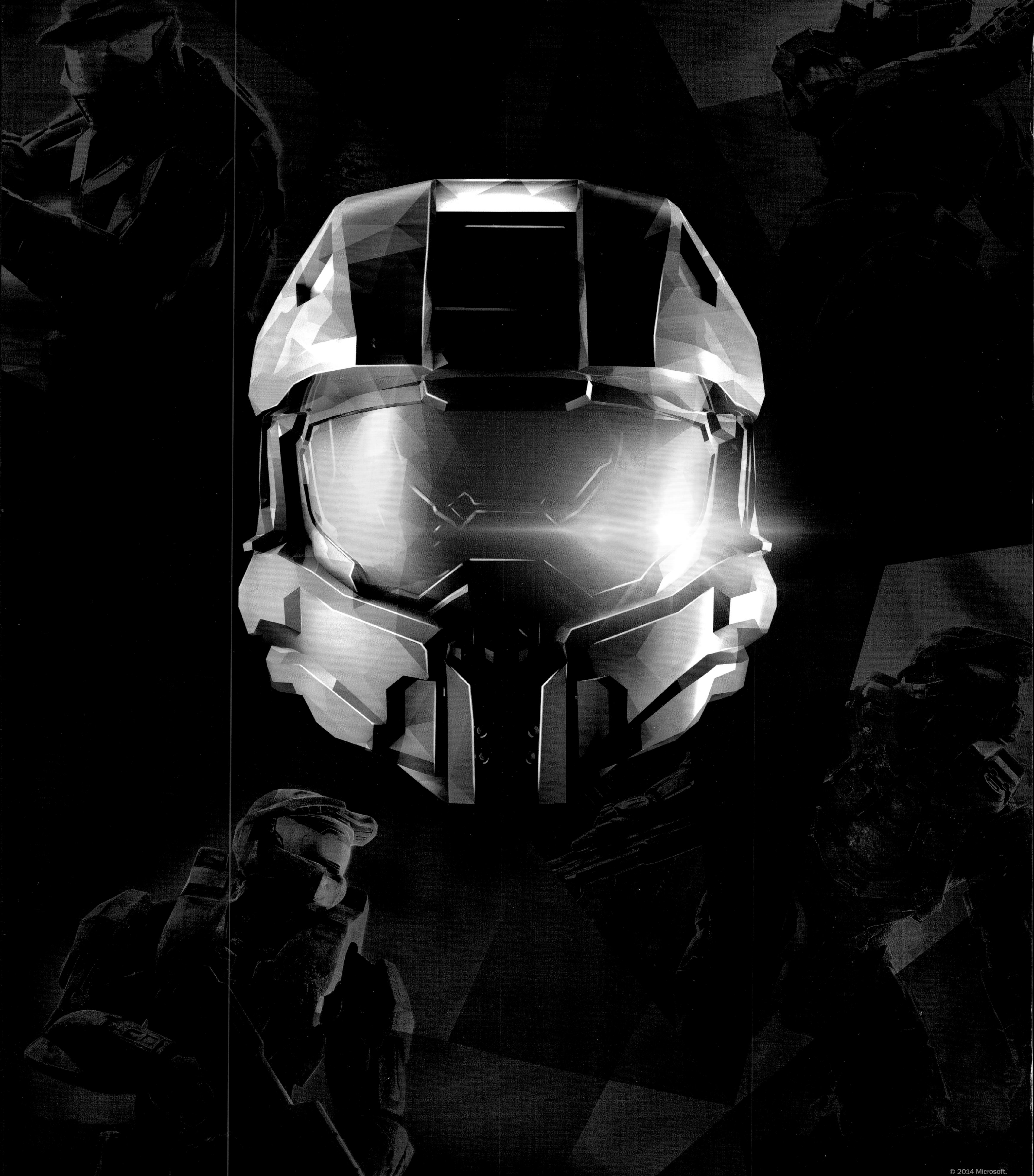

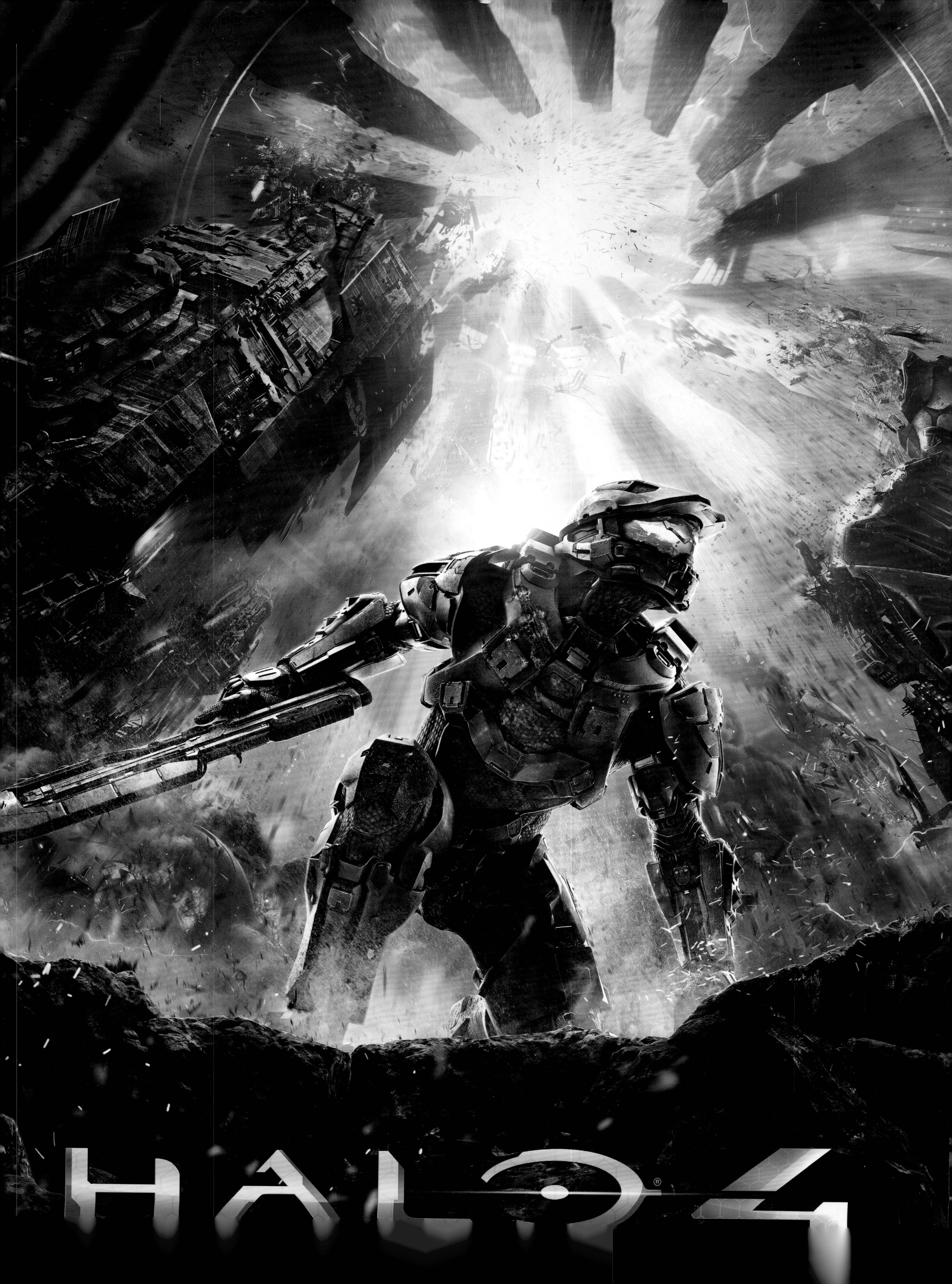
HALO 4

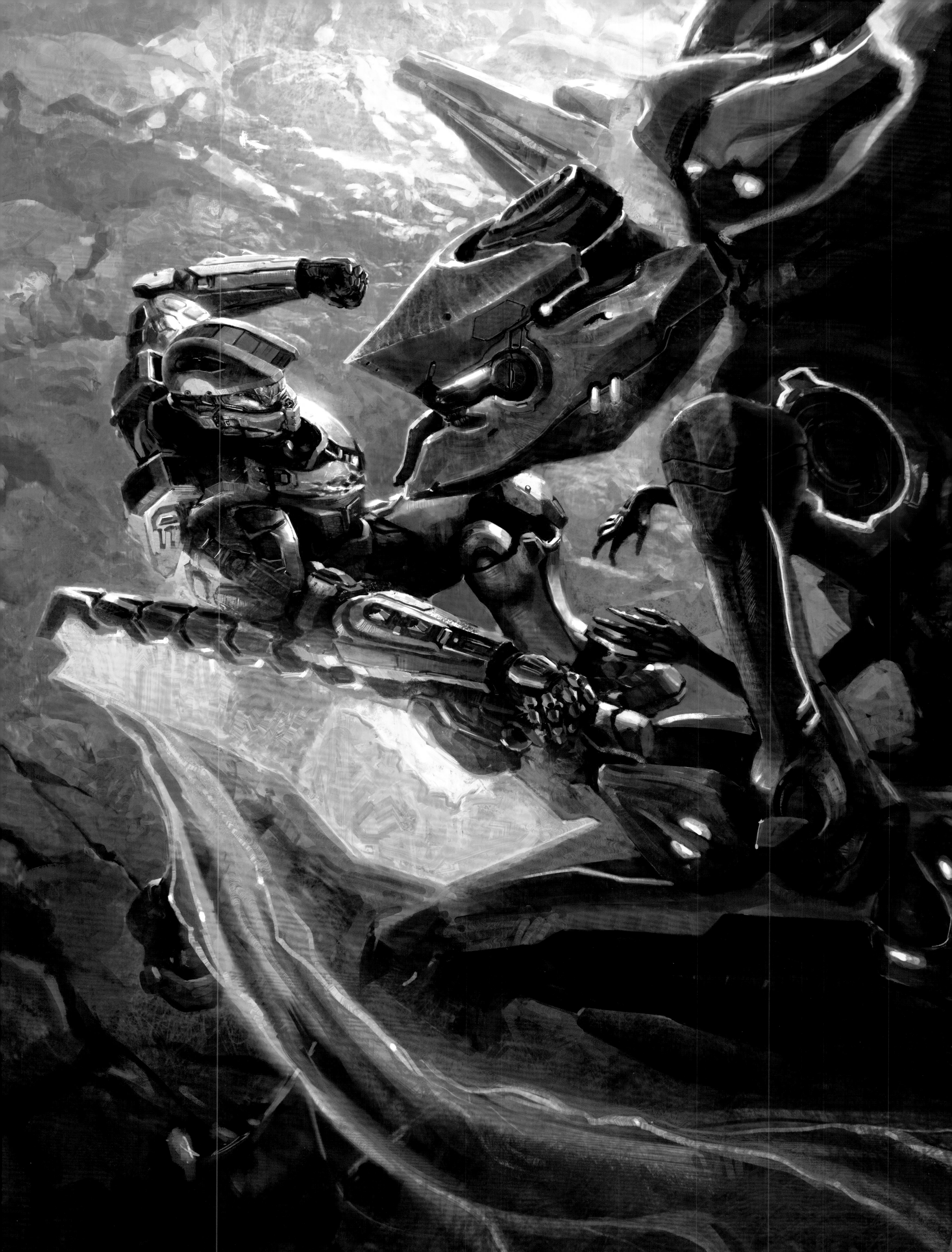

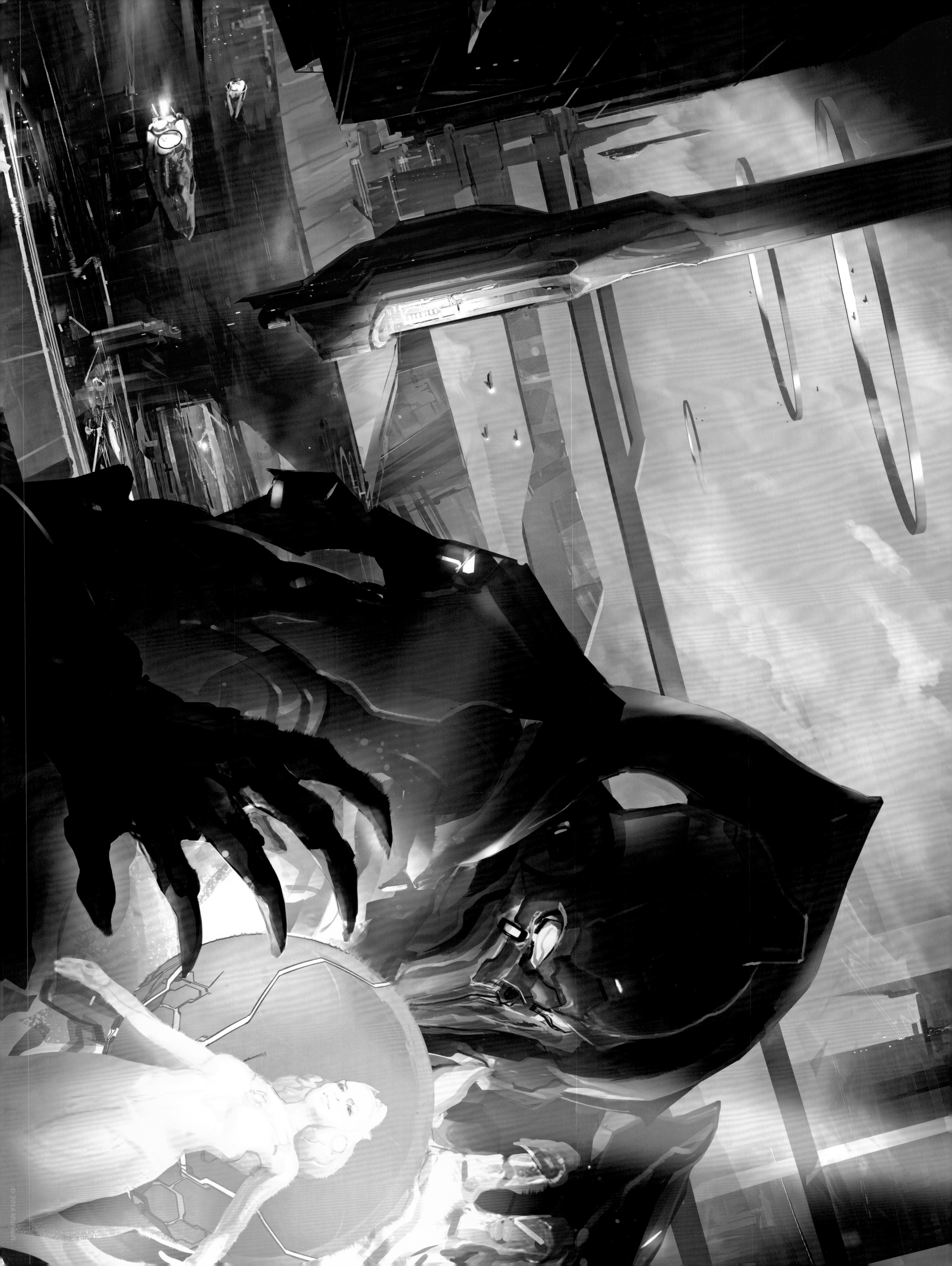

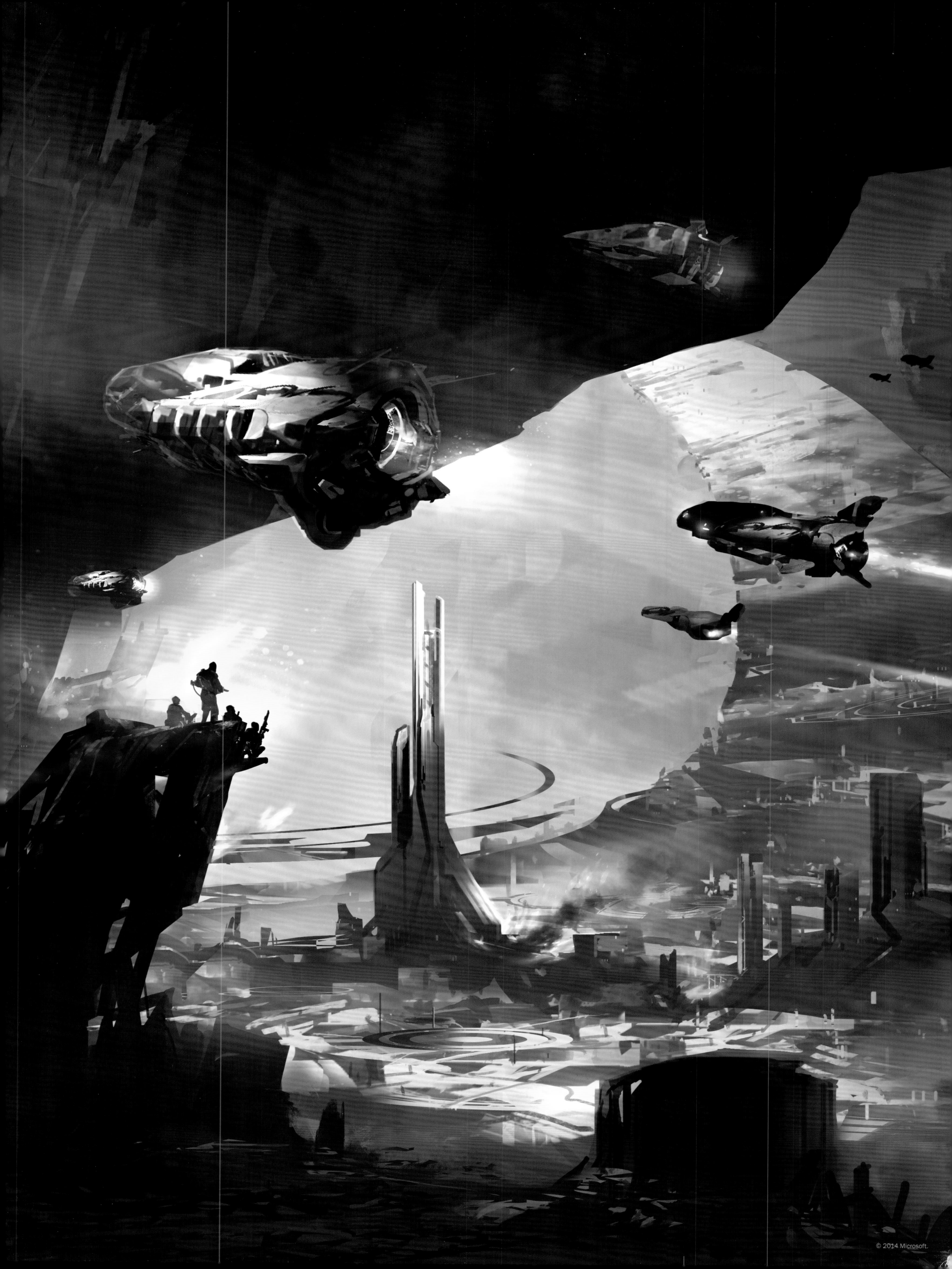

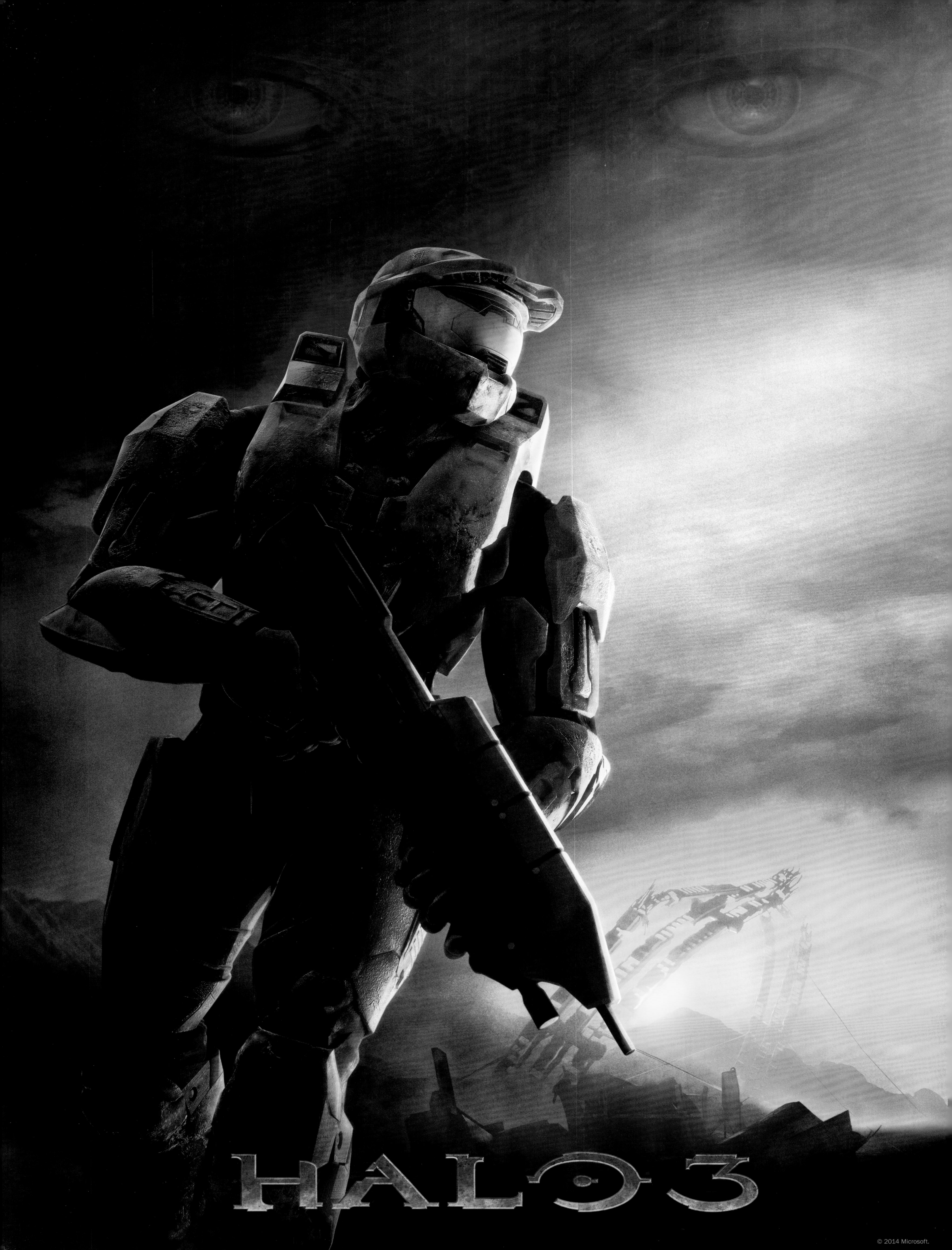
HALO 3

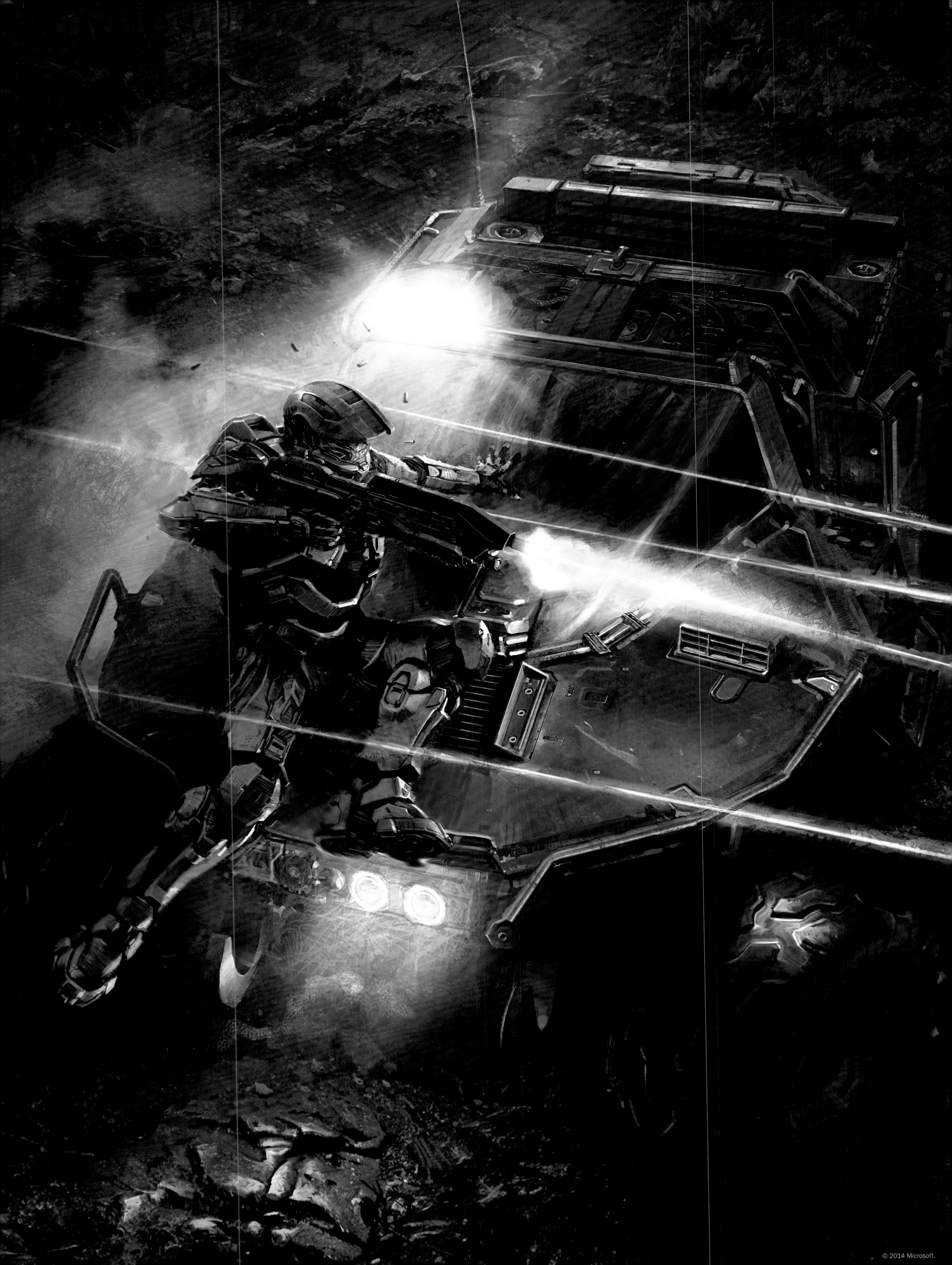

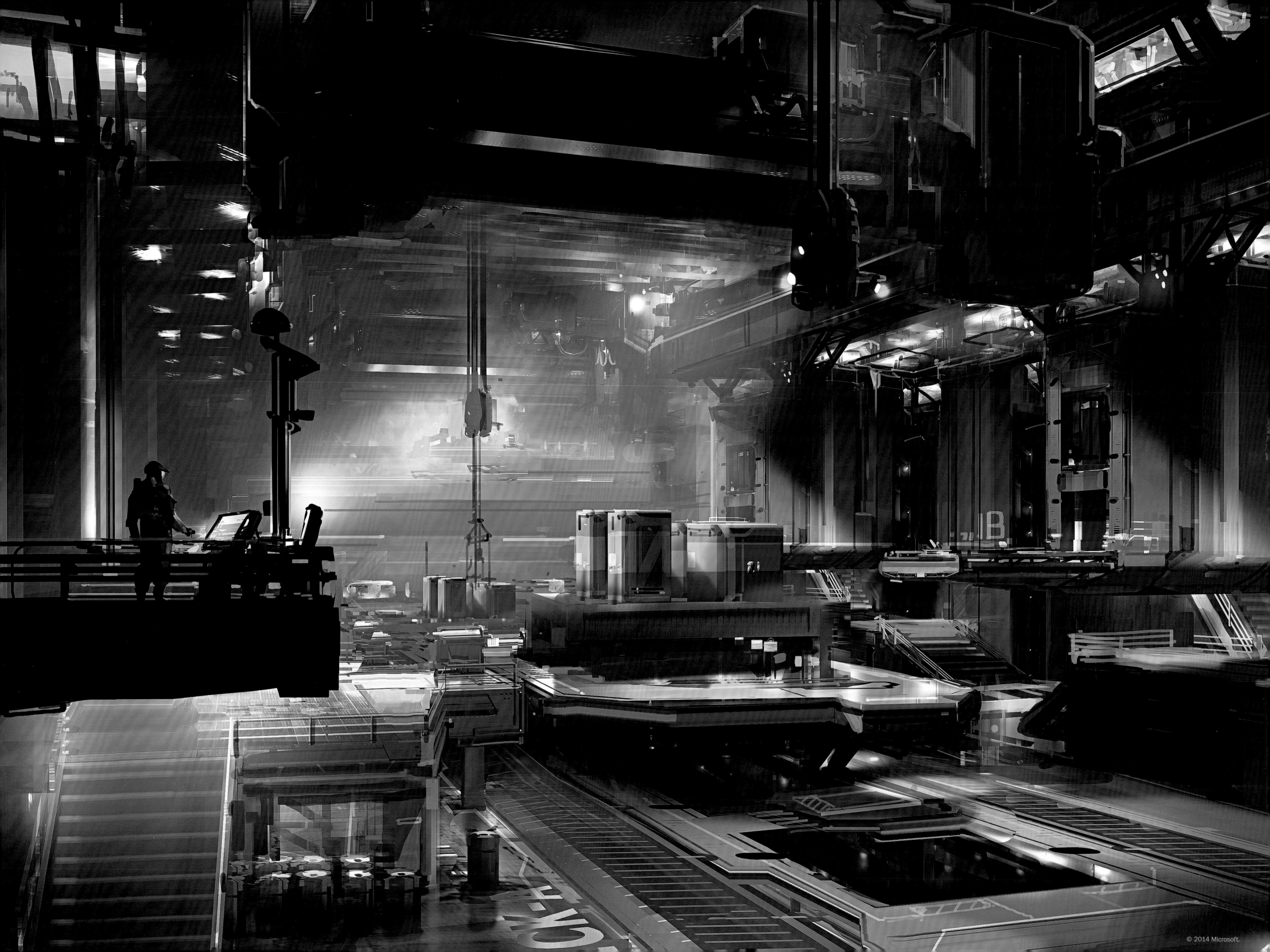

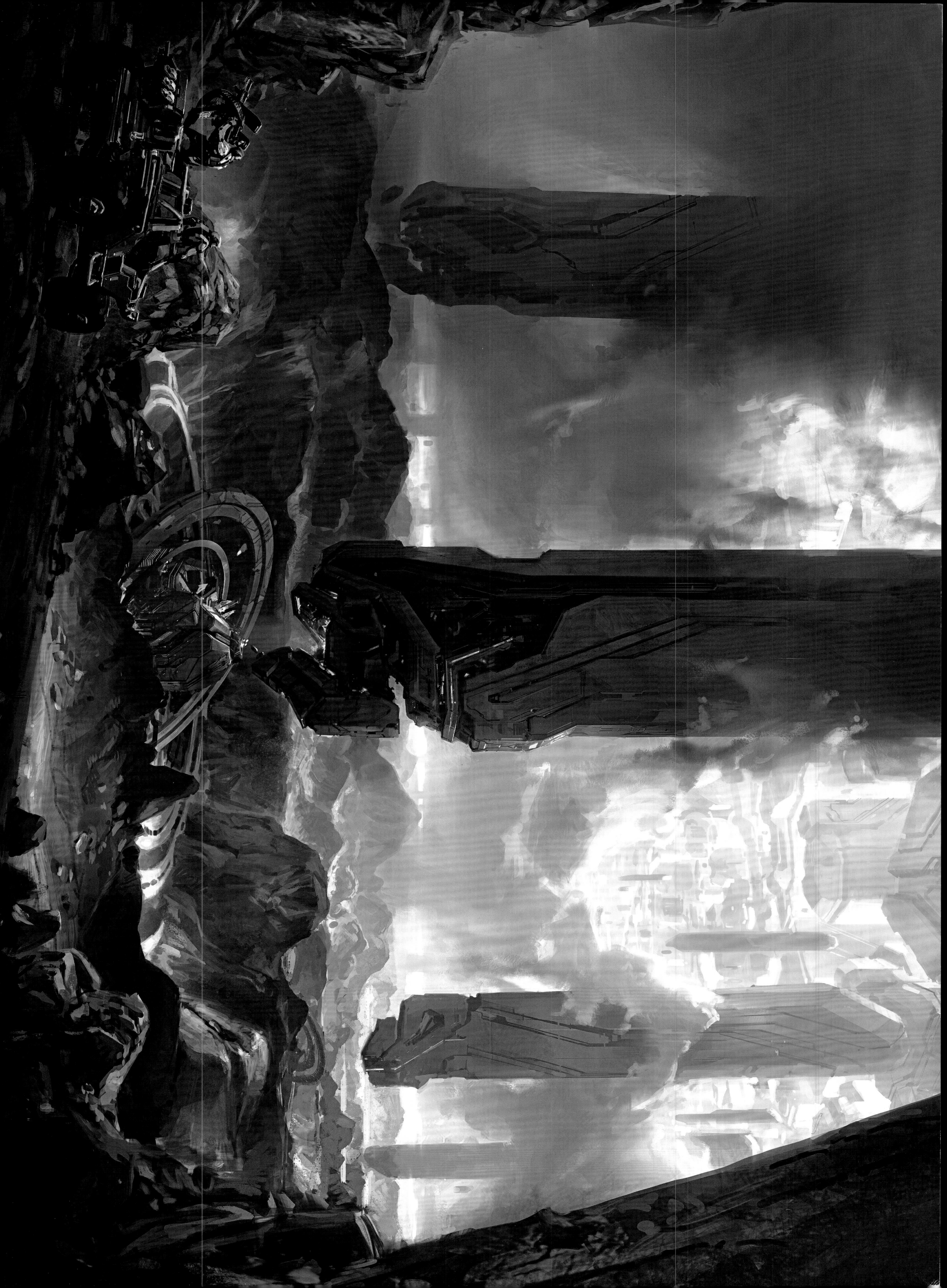

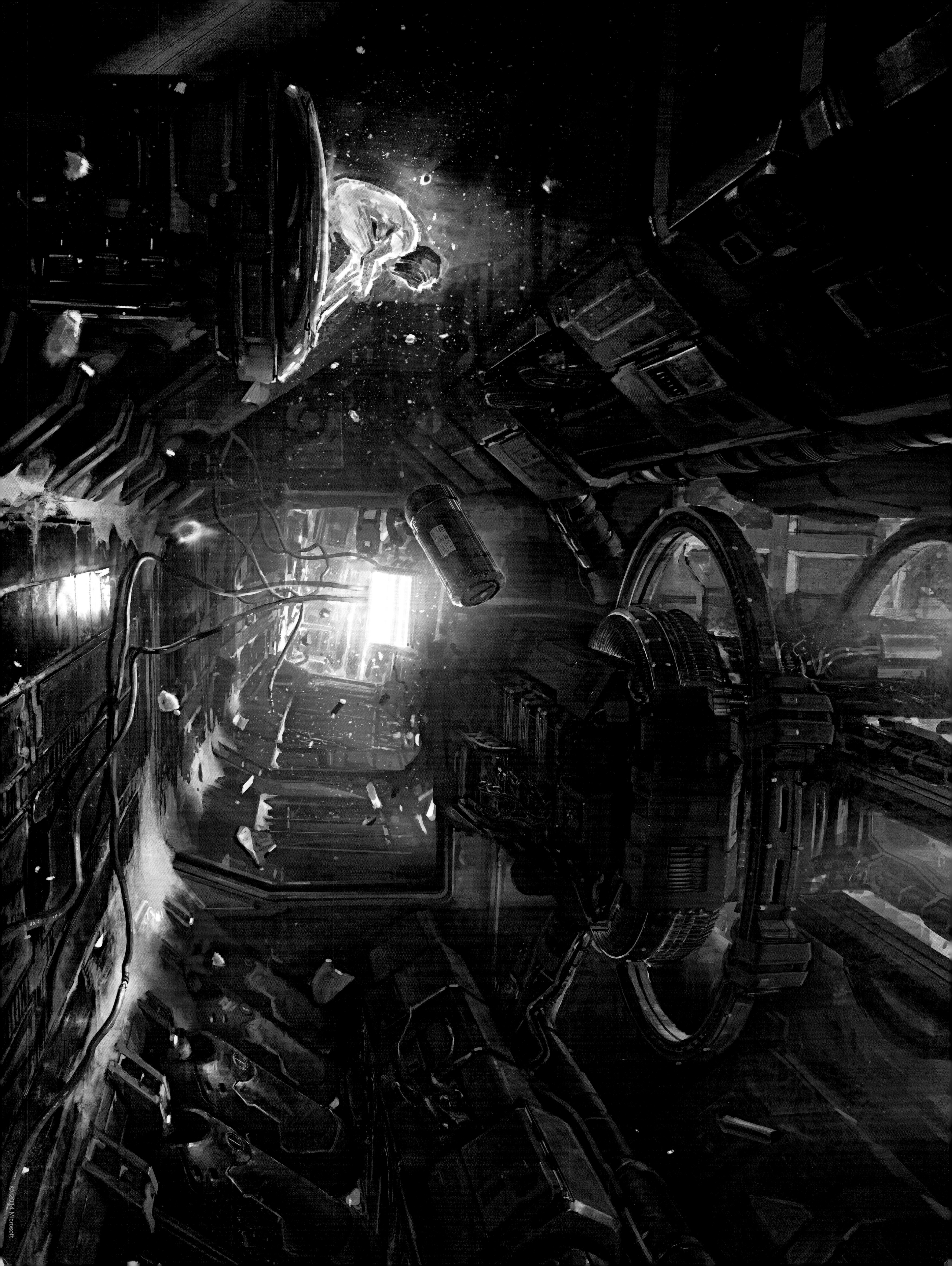

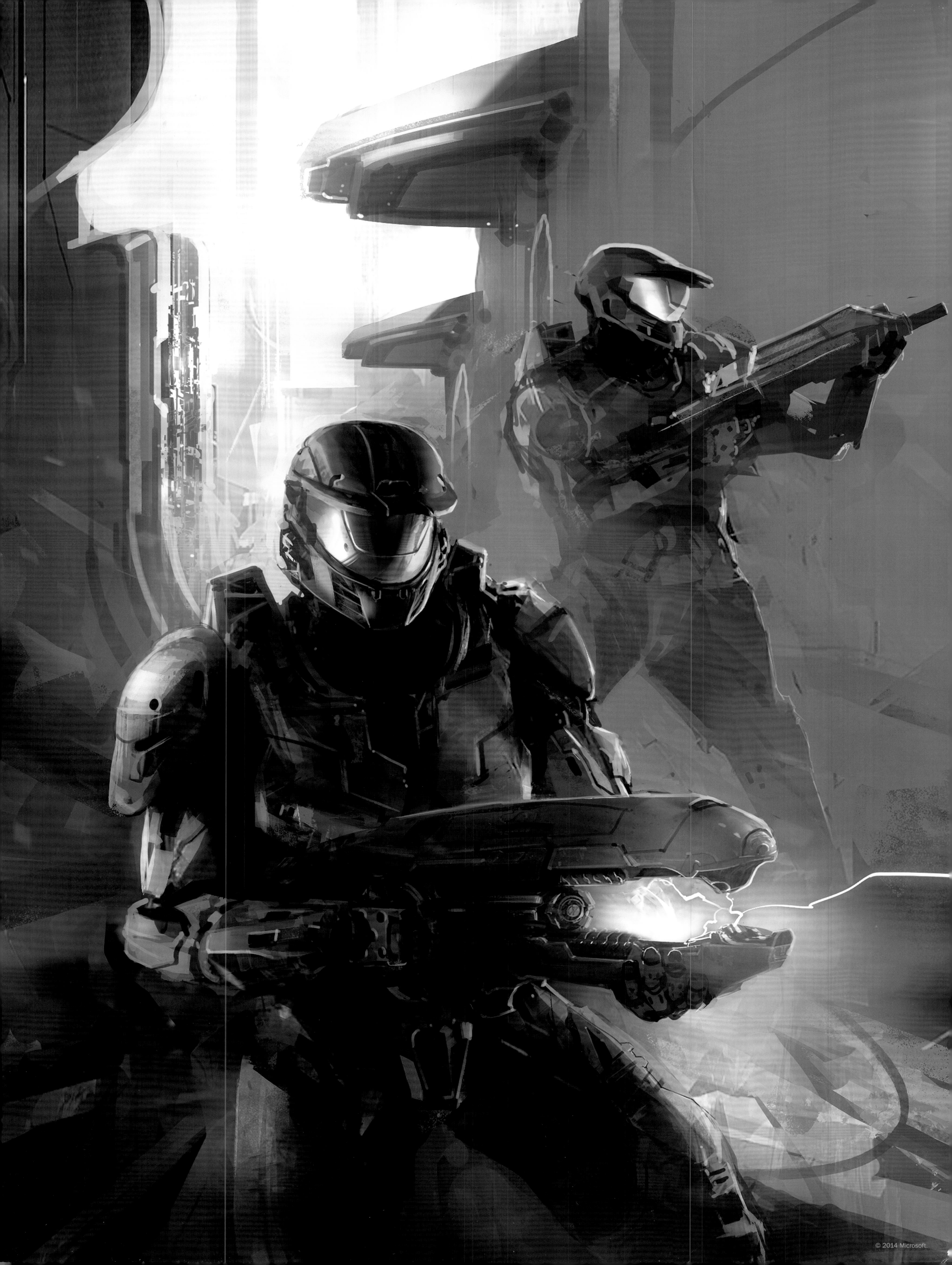

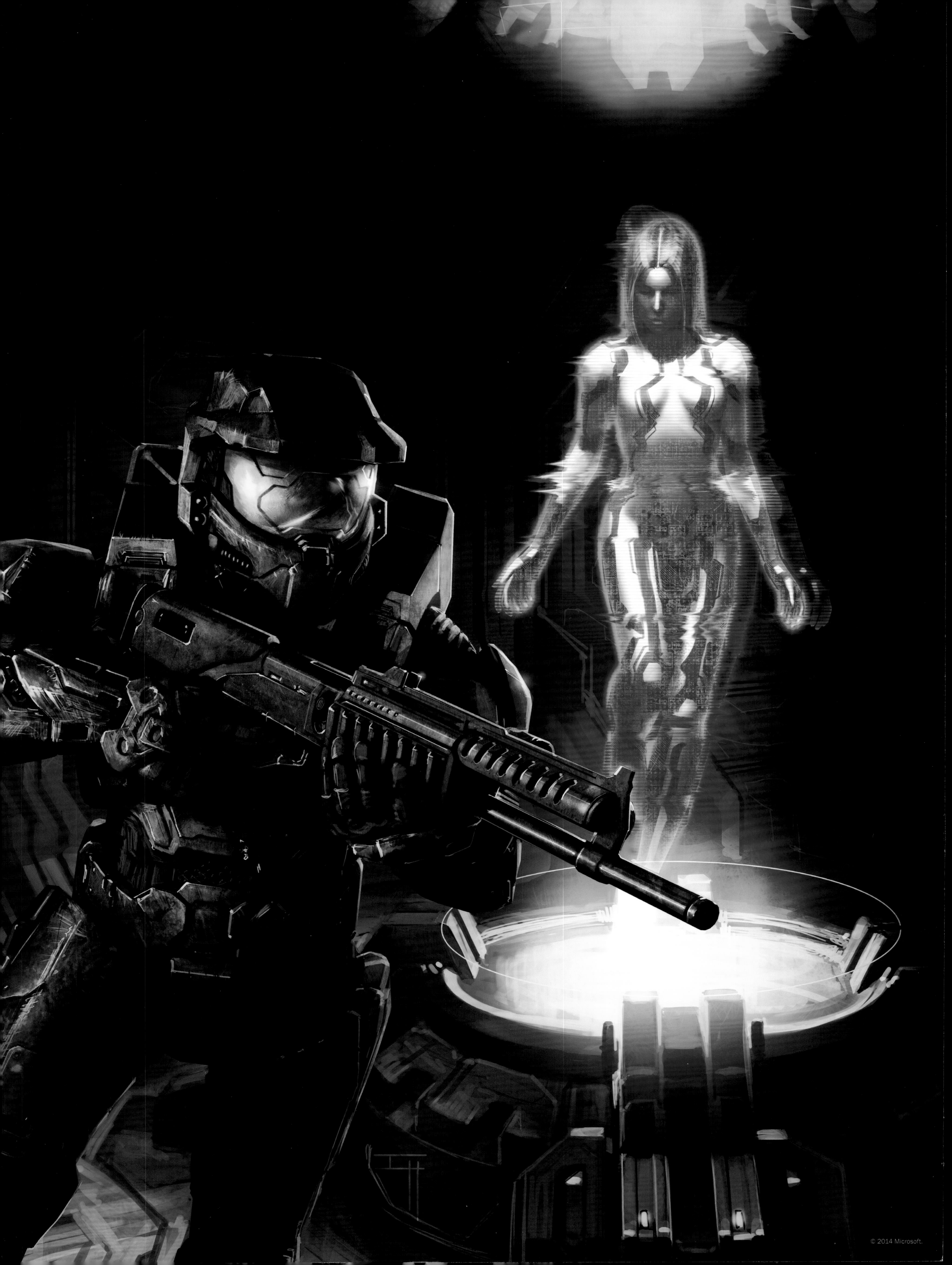

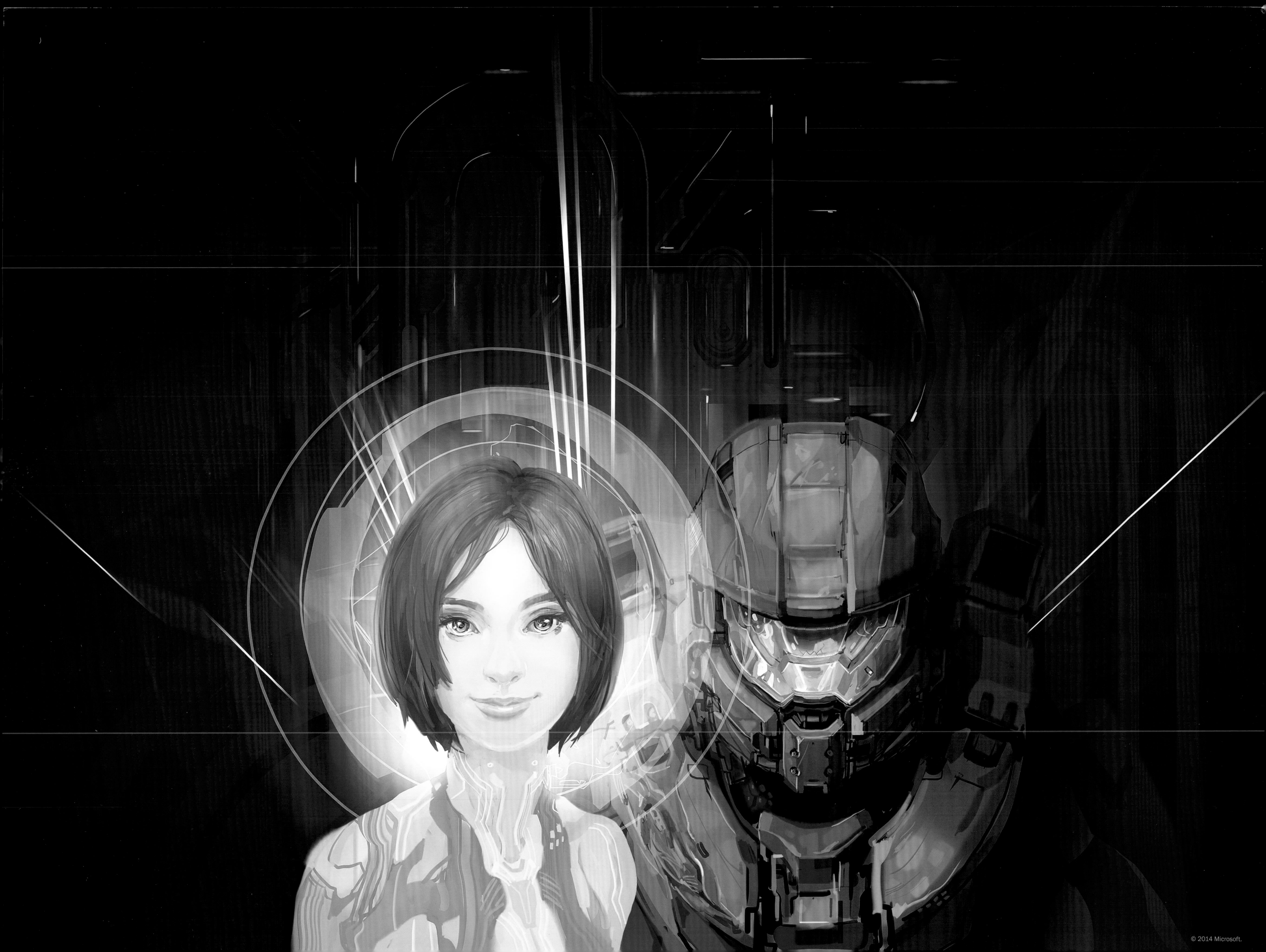

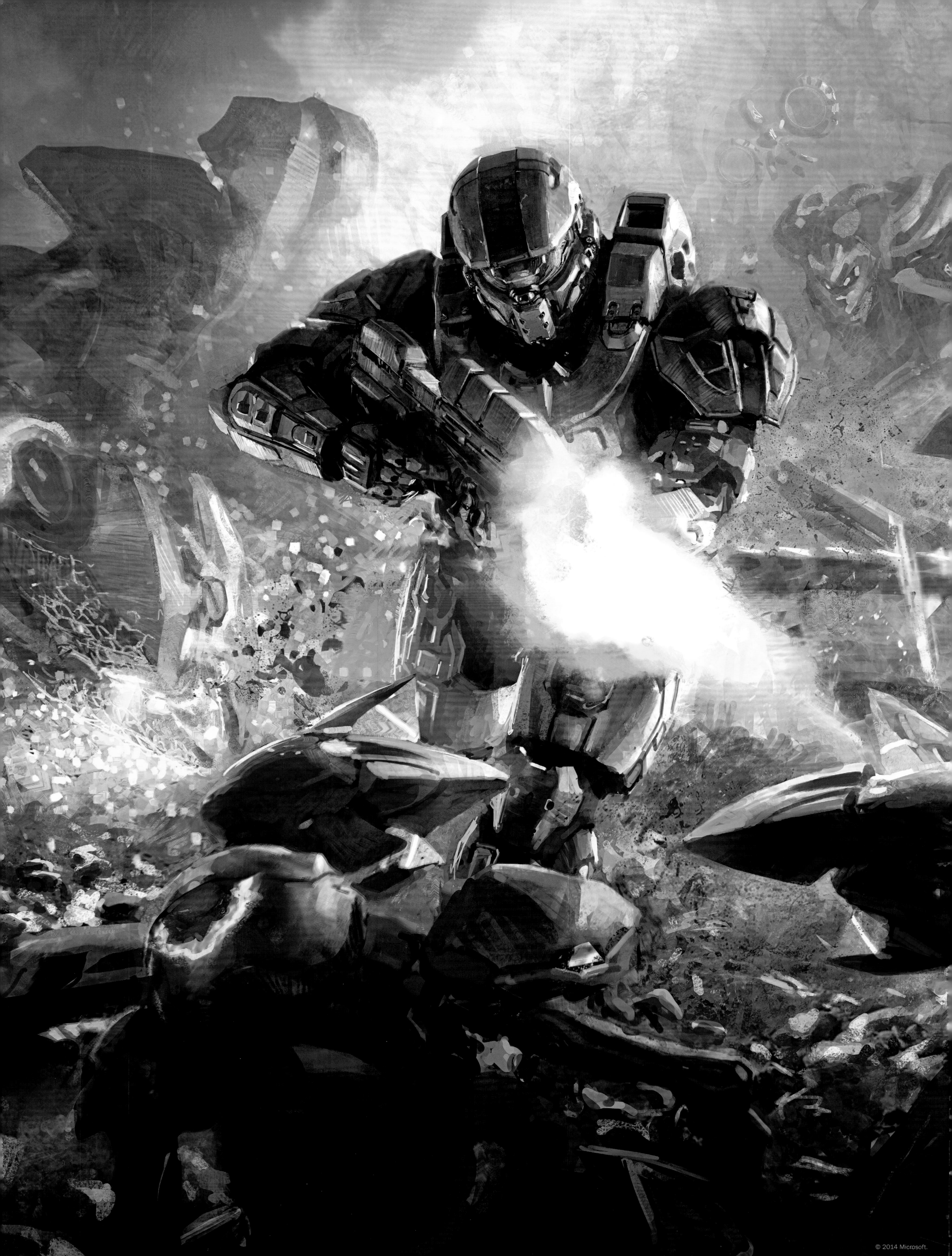

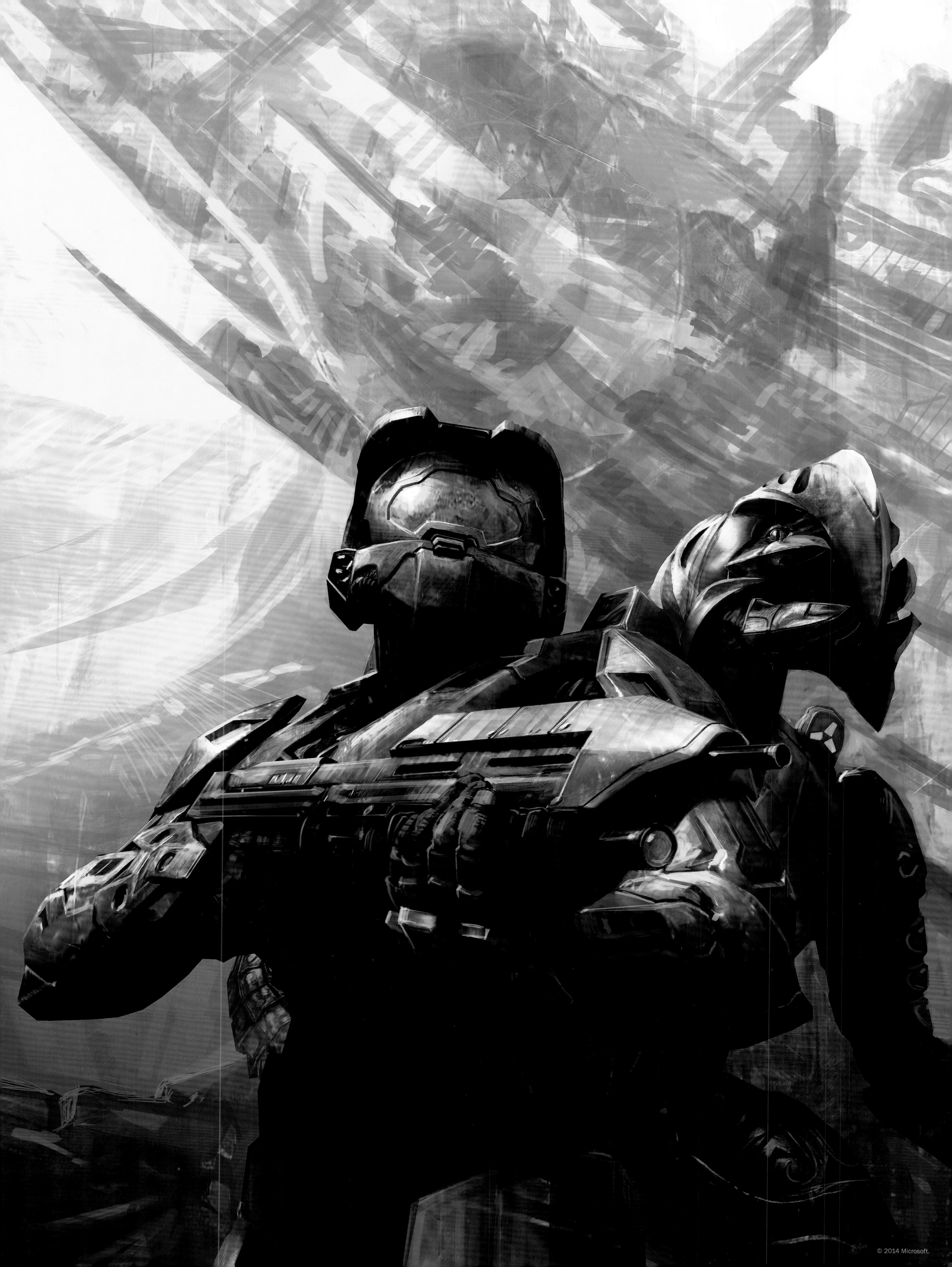

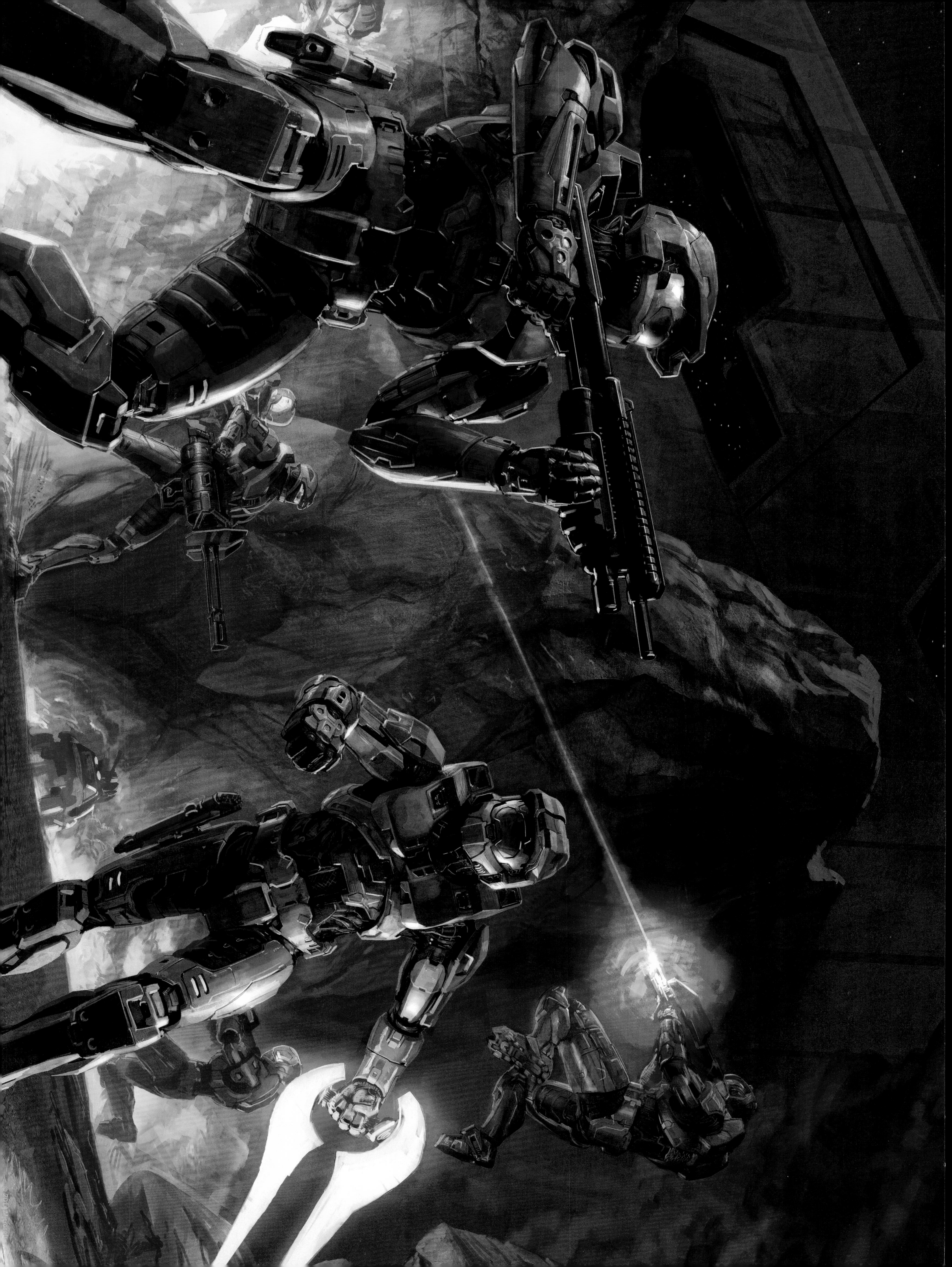

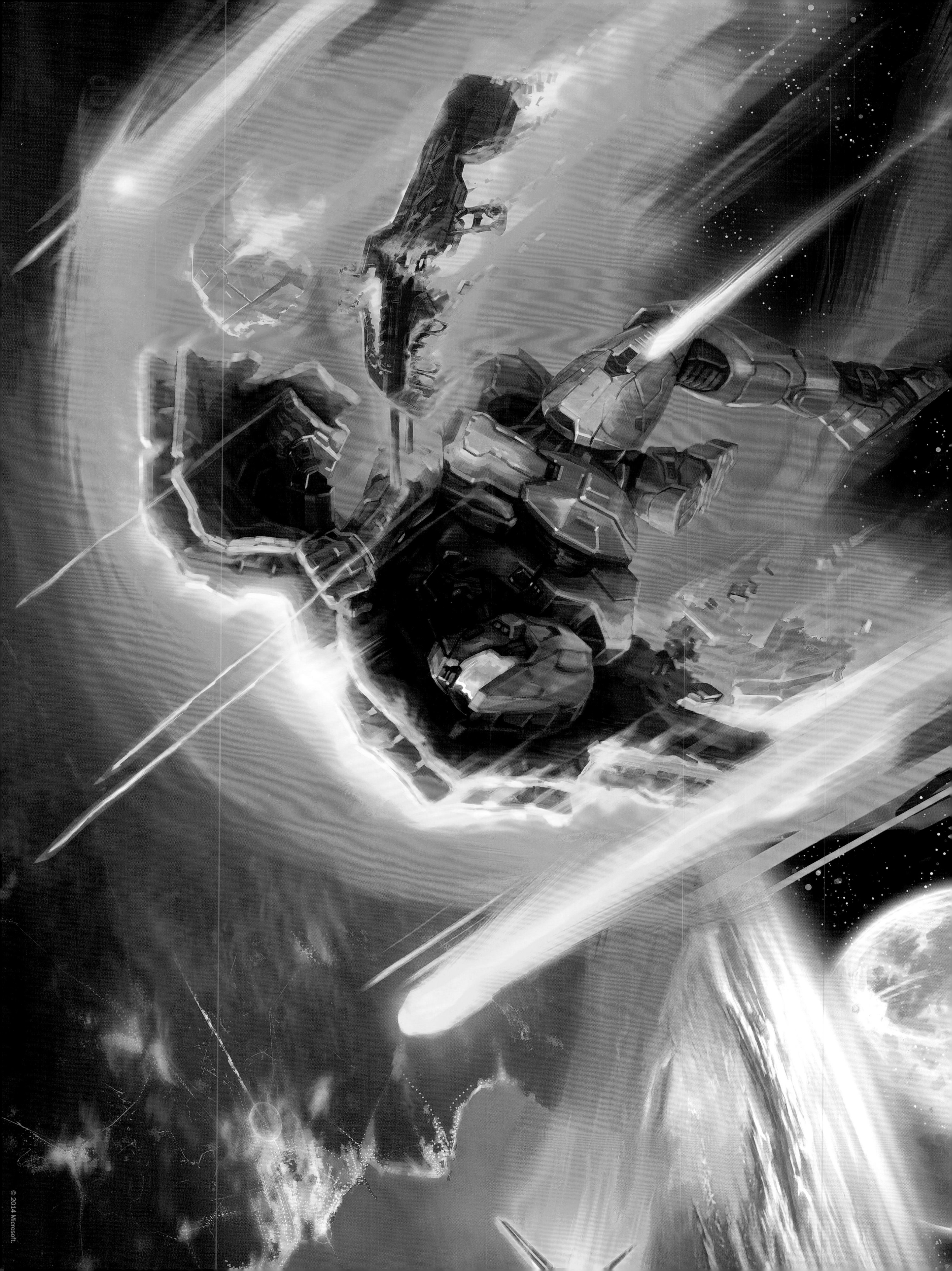

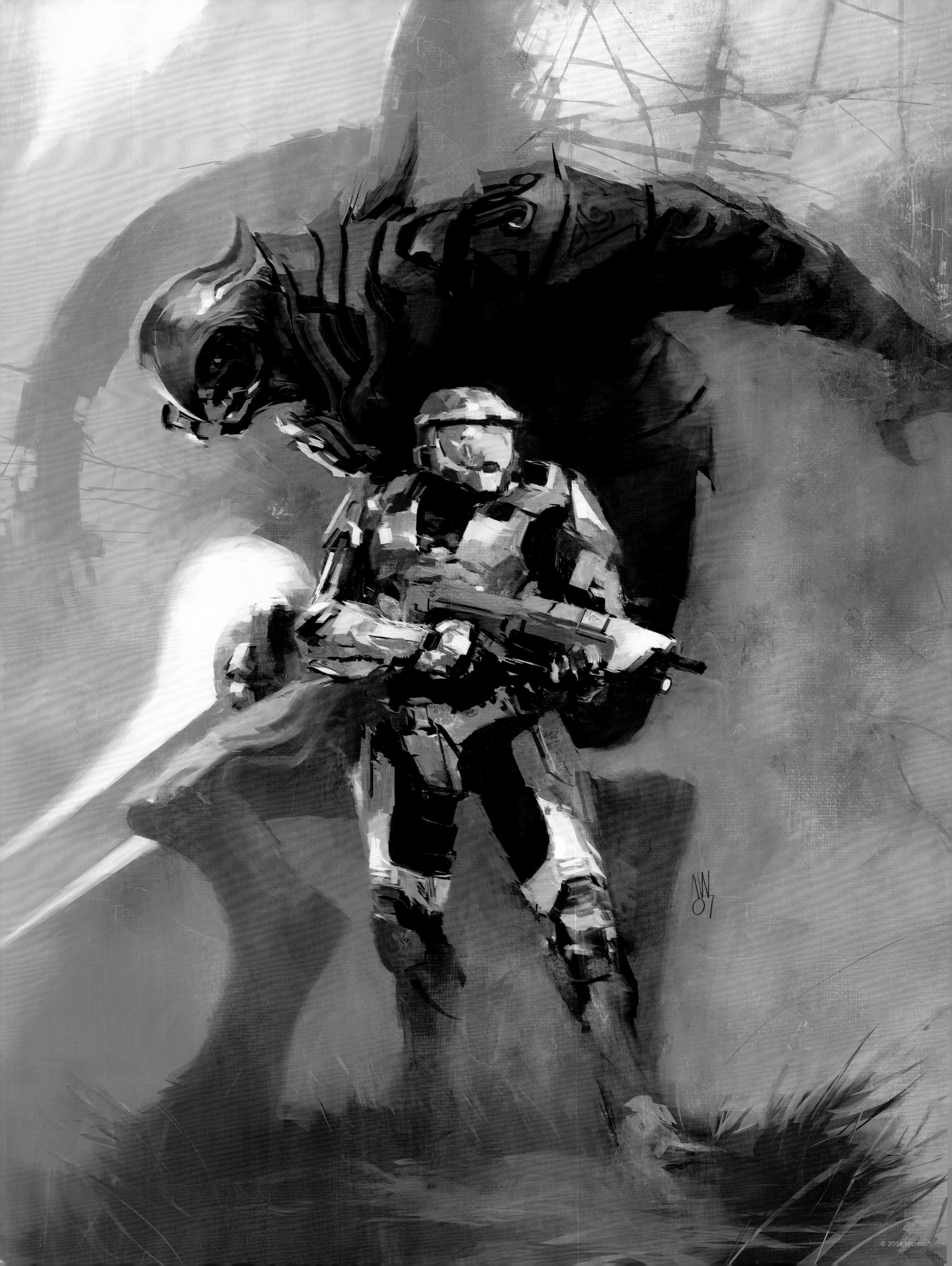

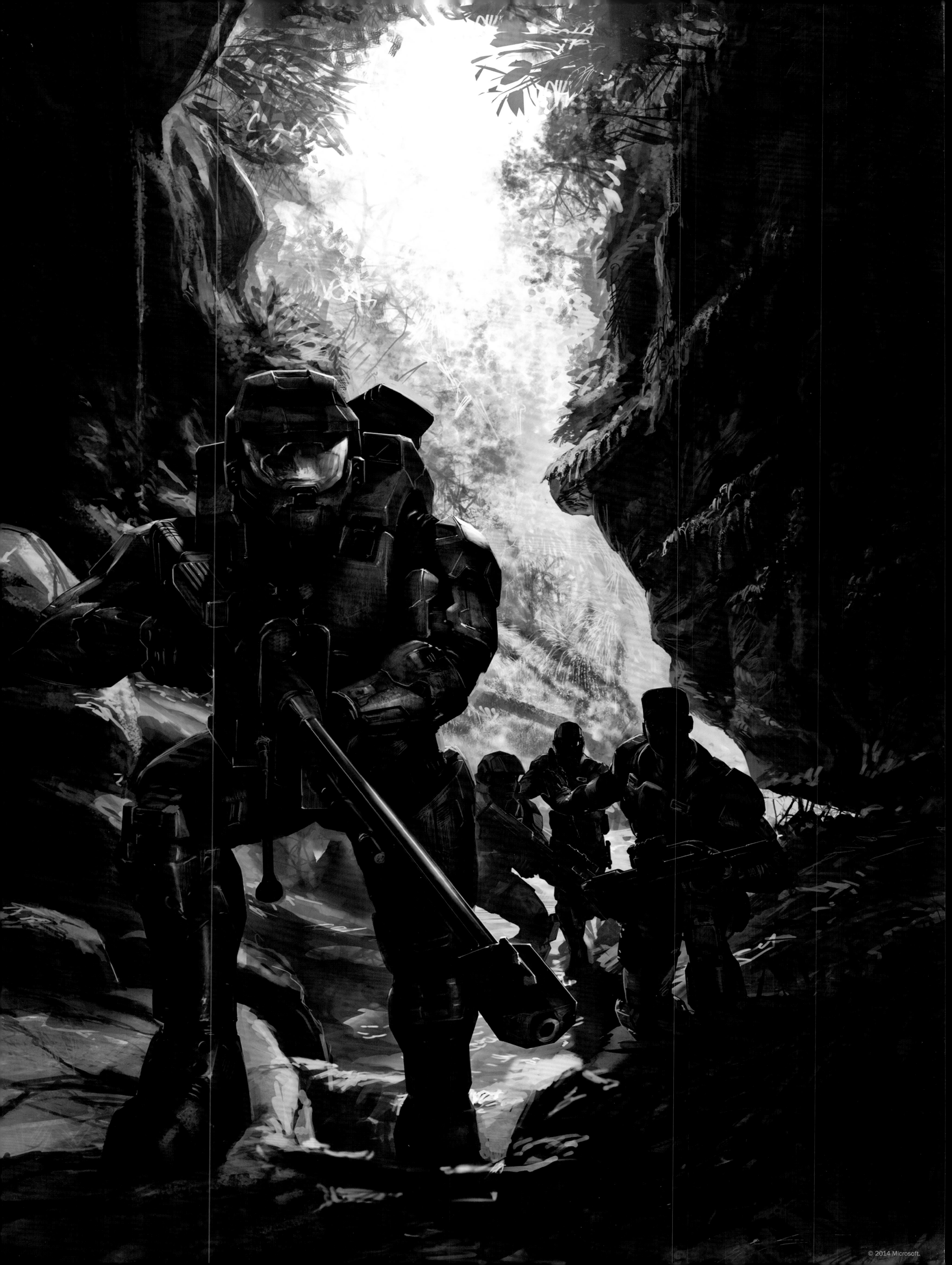

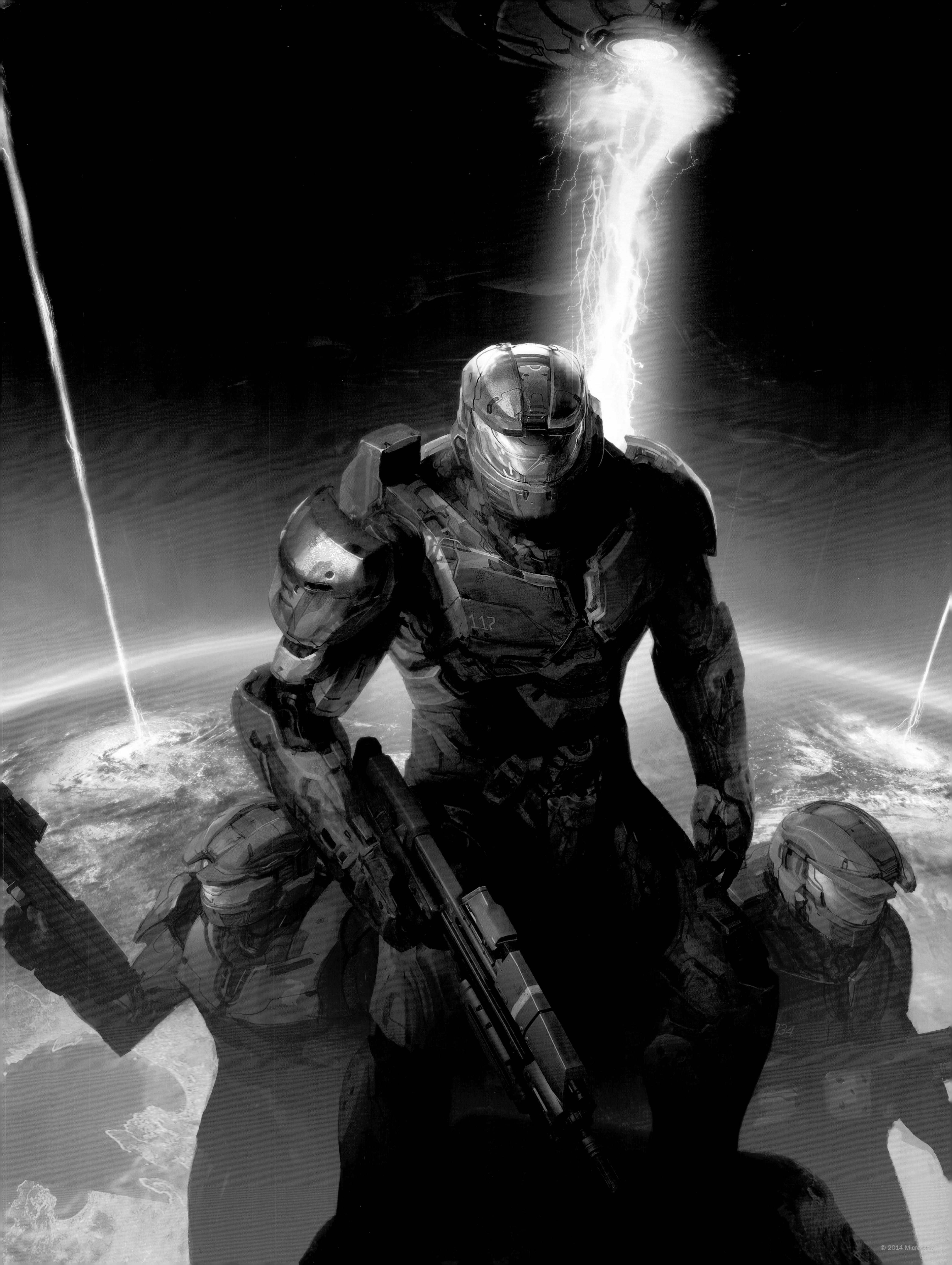
117

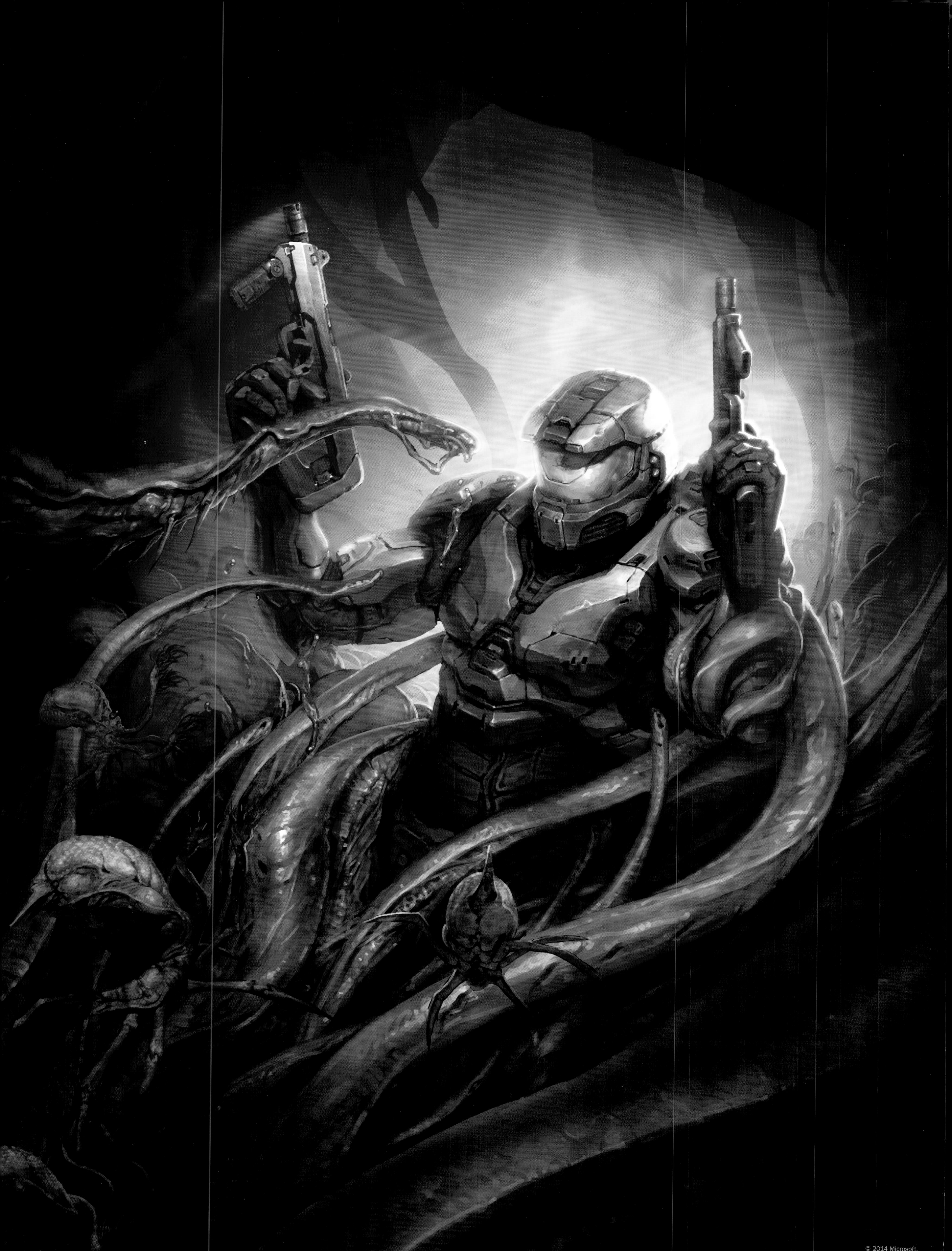

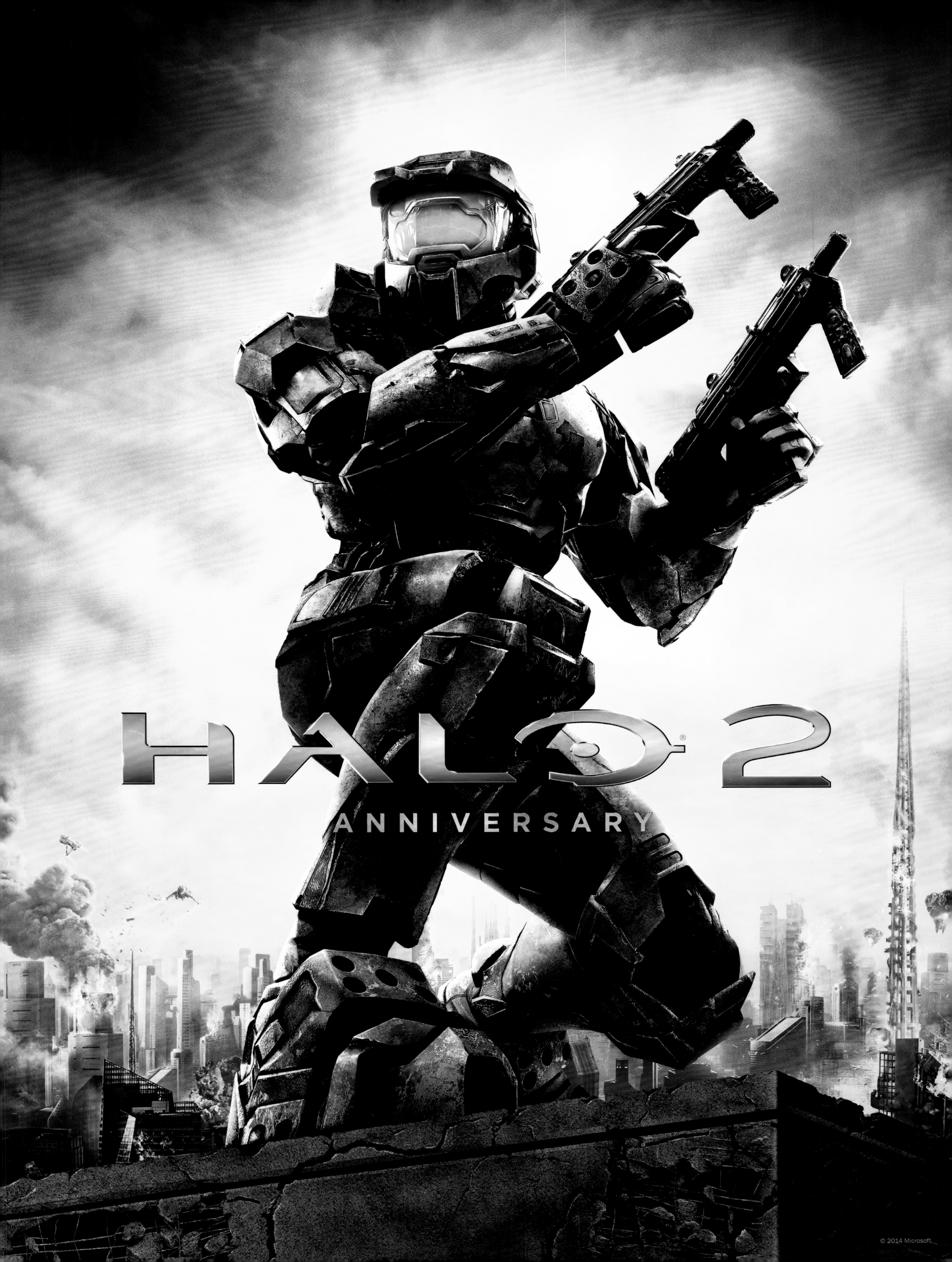
HALO 2
ANNIVERSARY
© 2014 Microsoft.

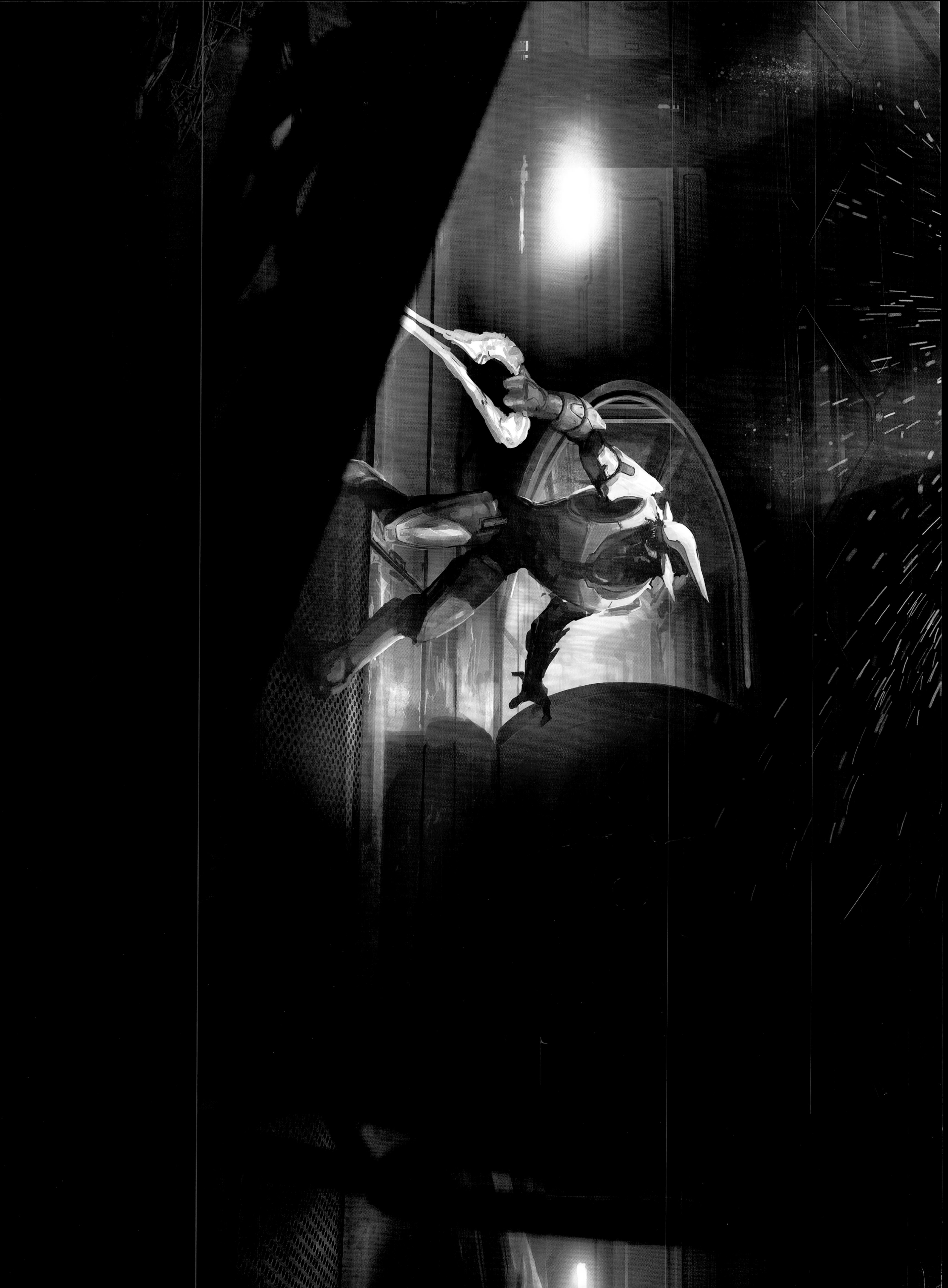

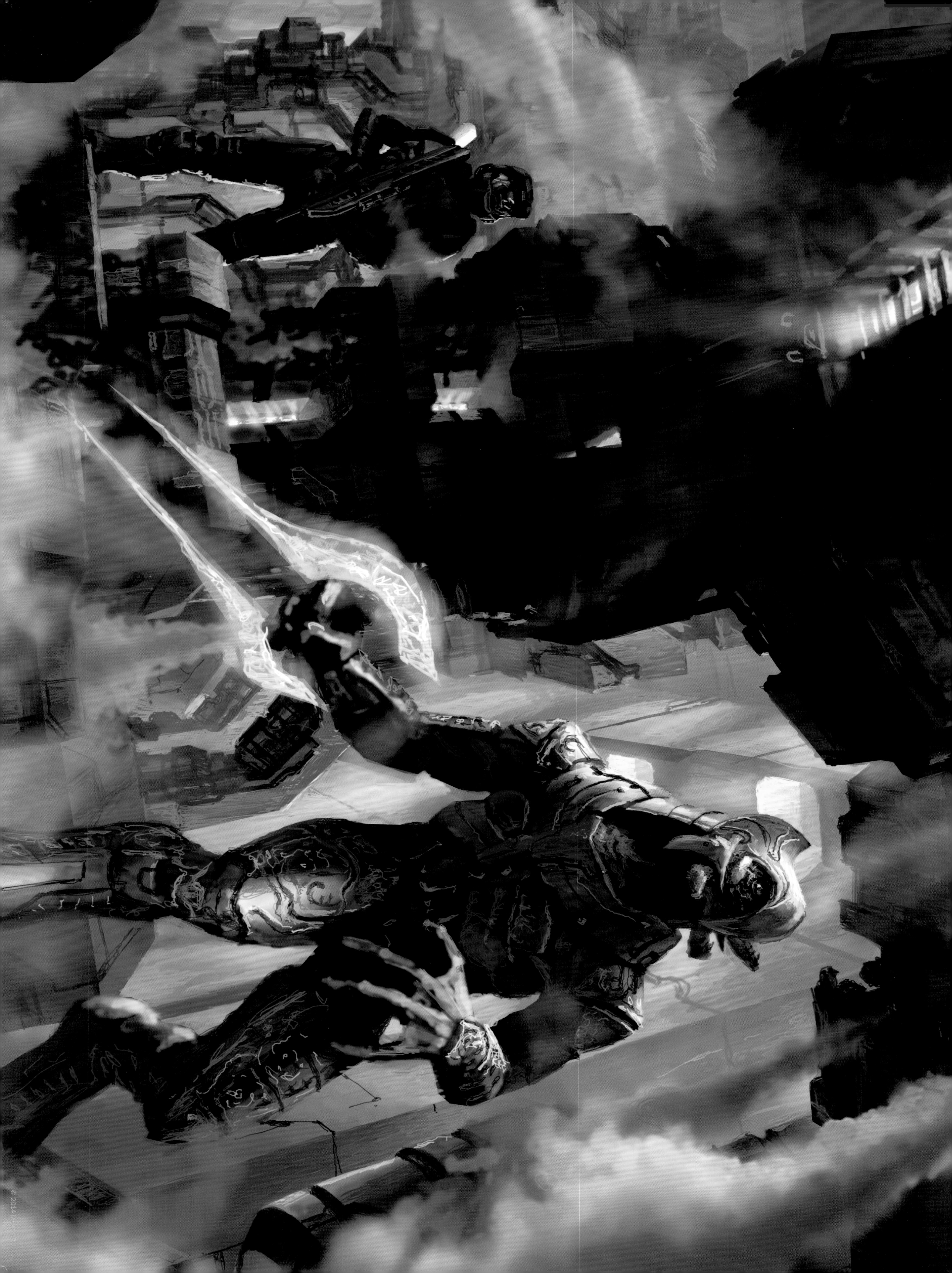

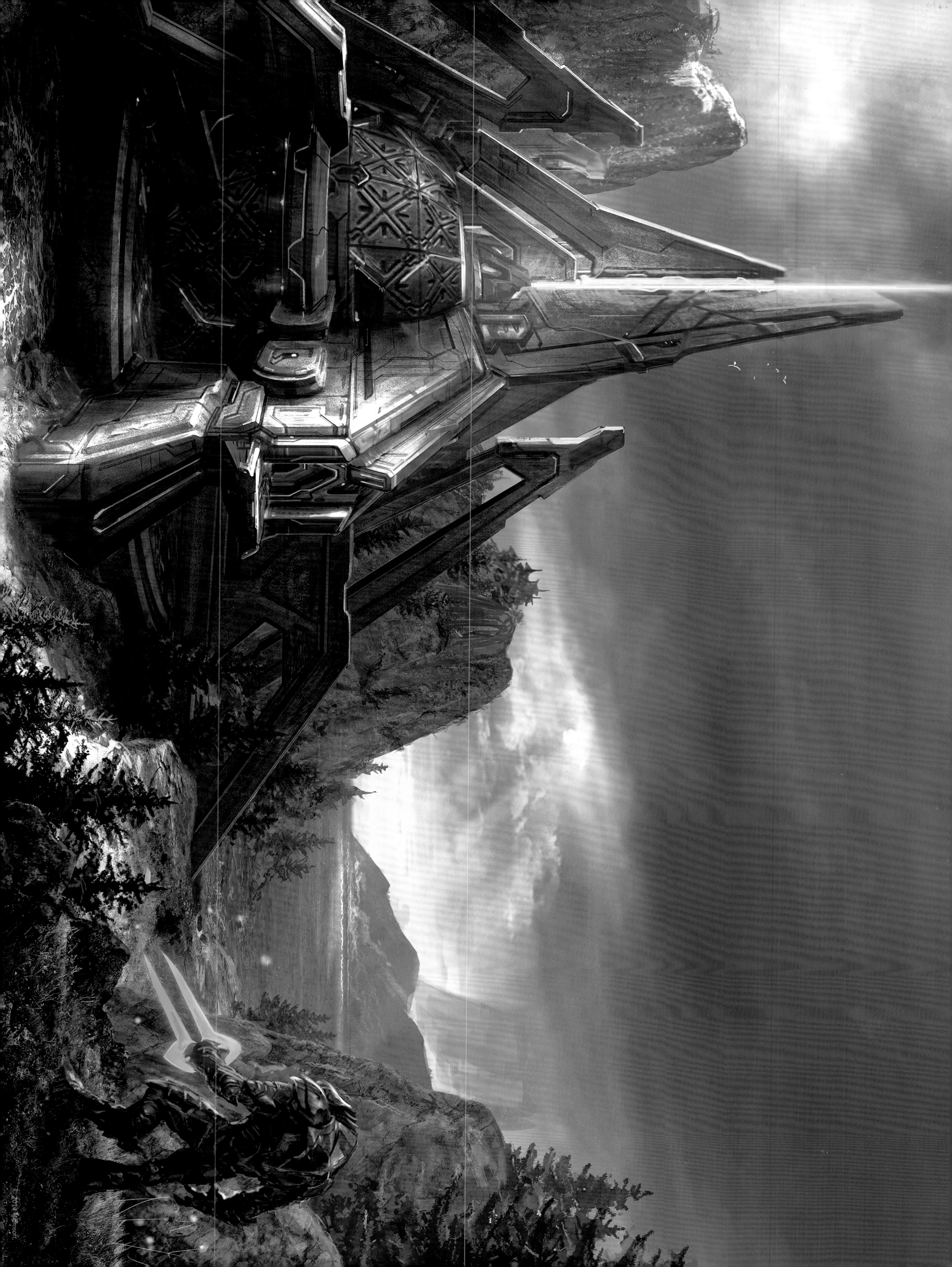

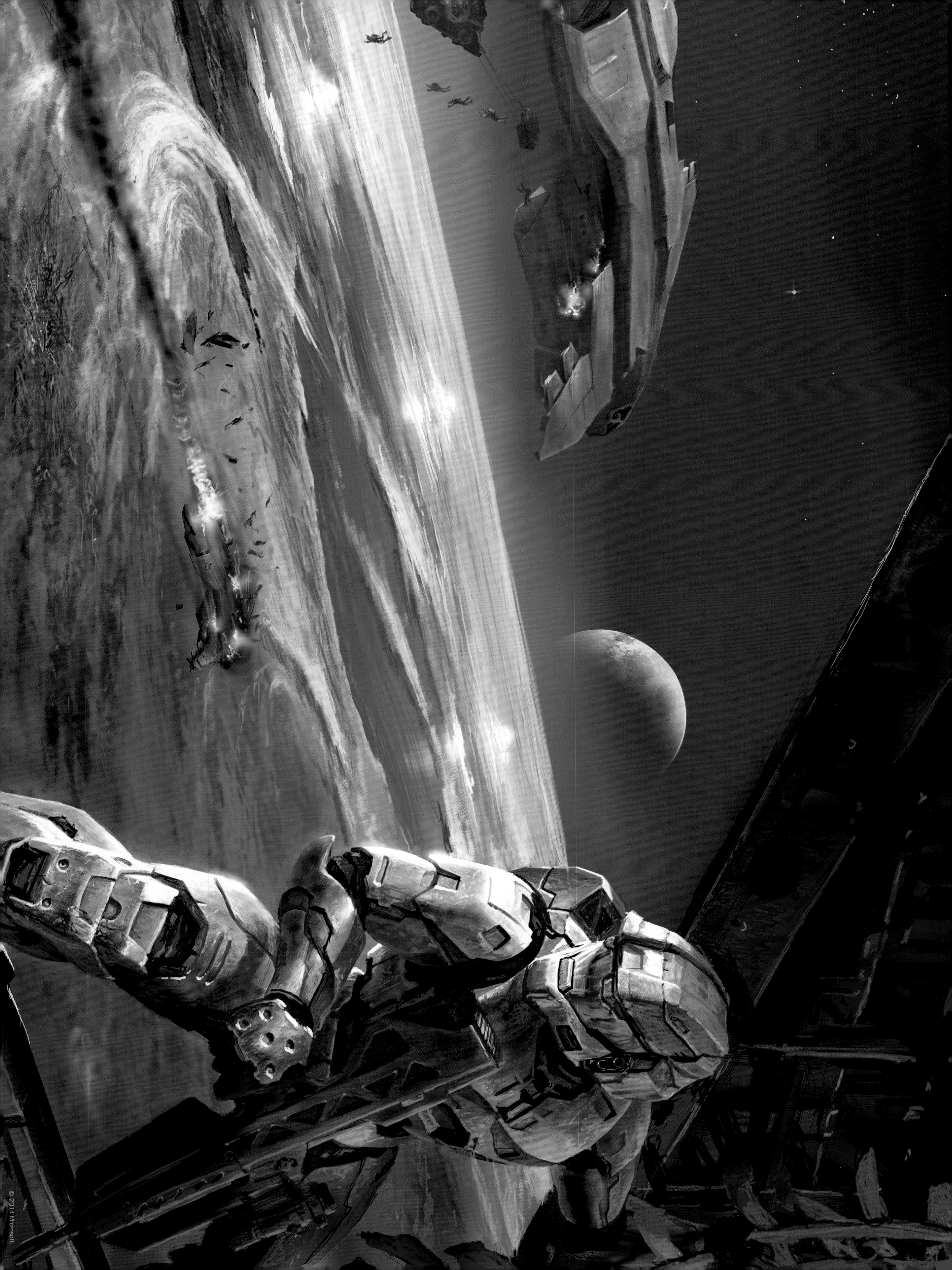

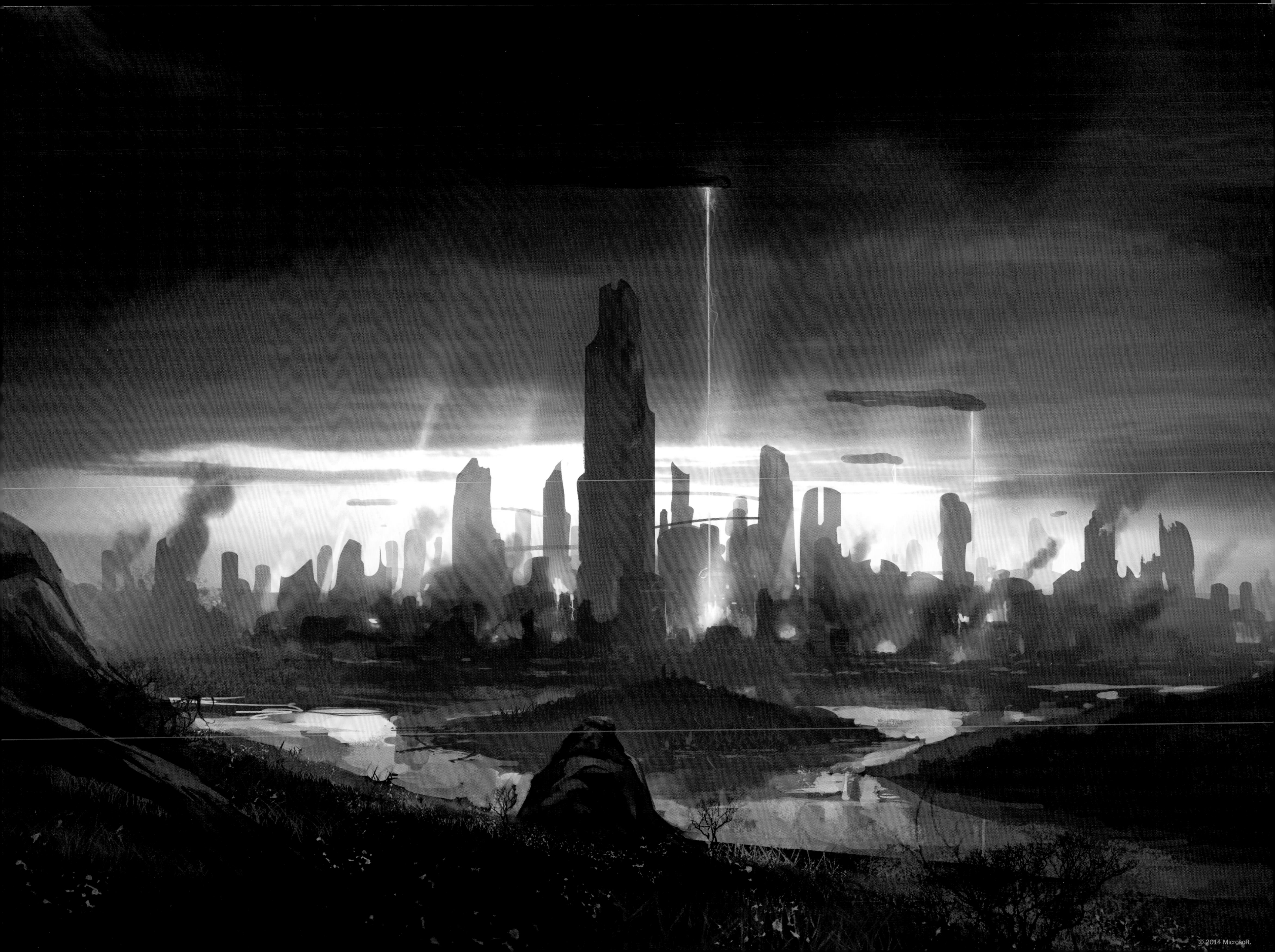

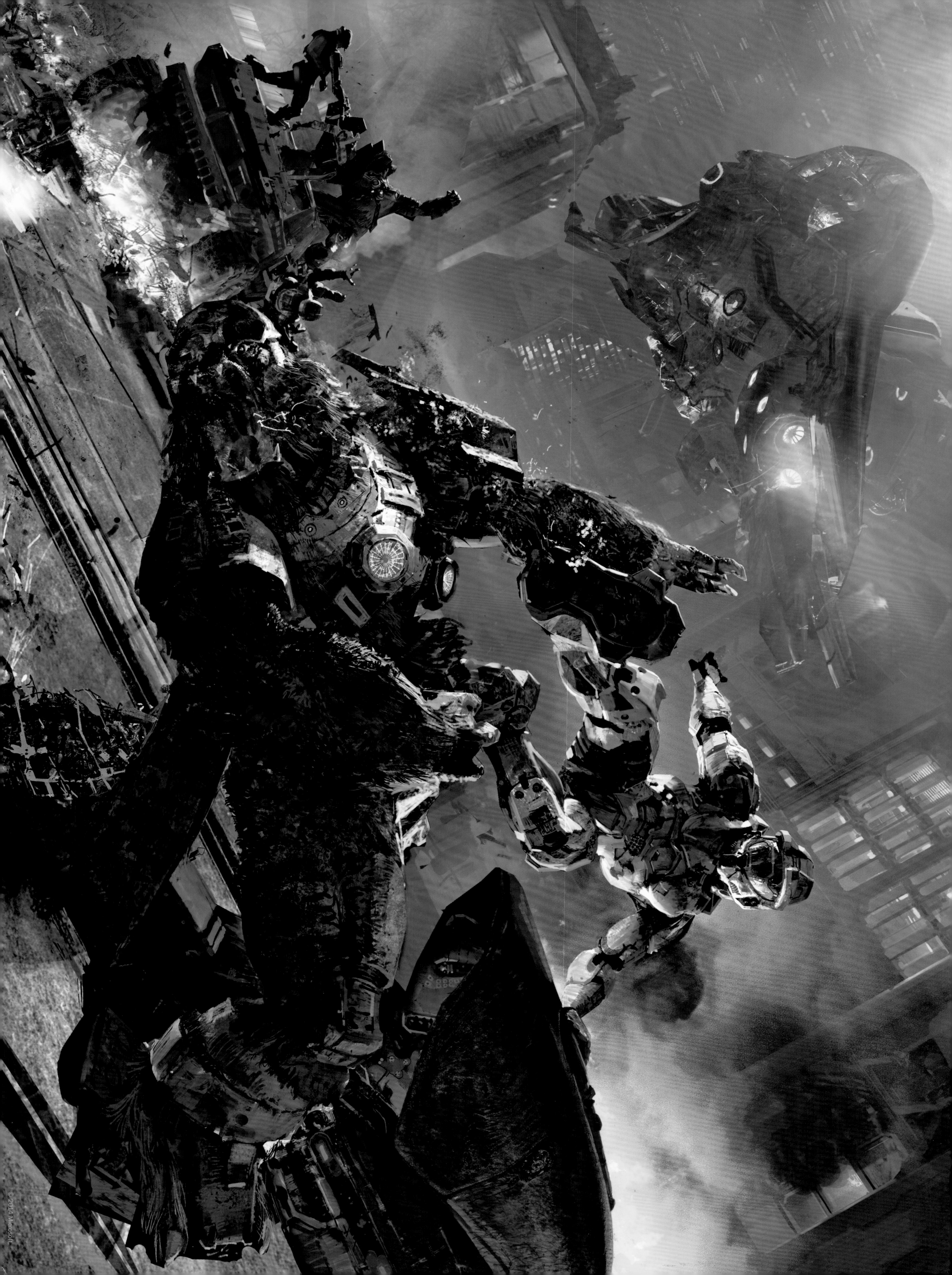

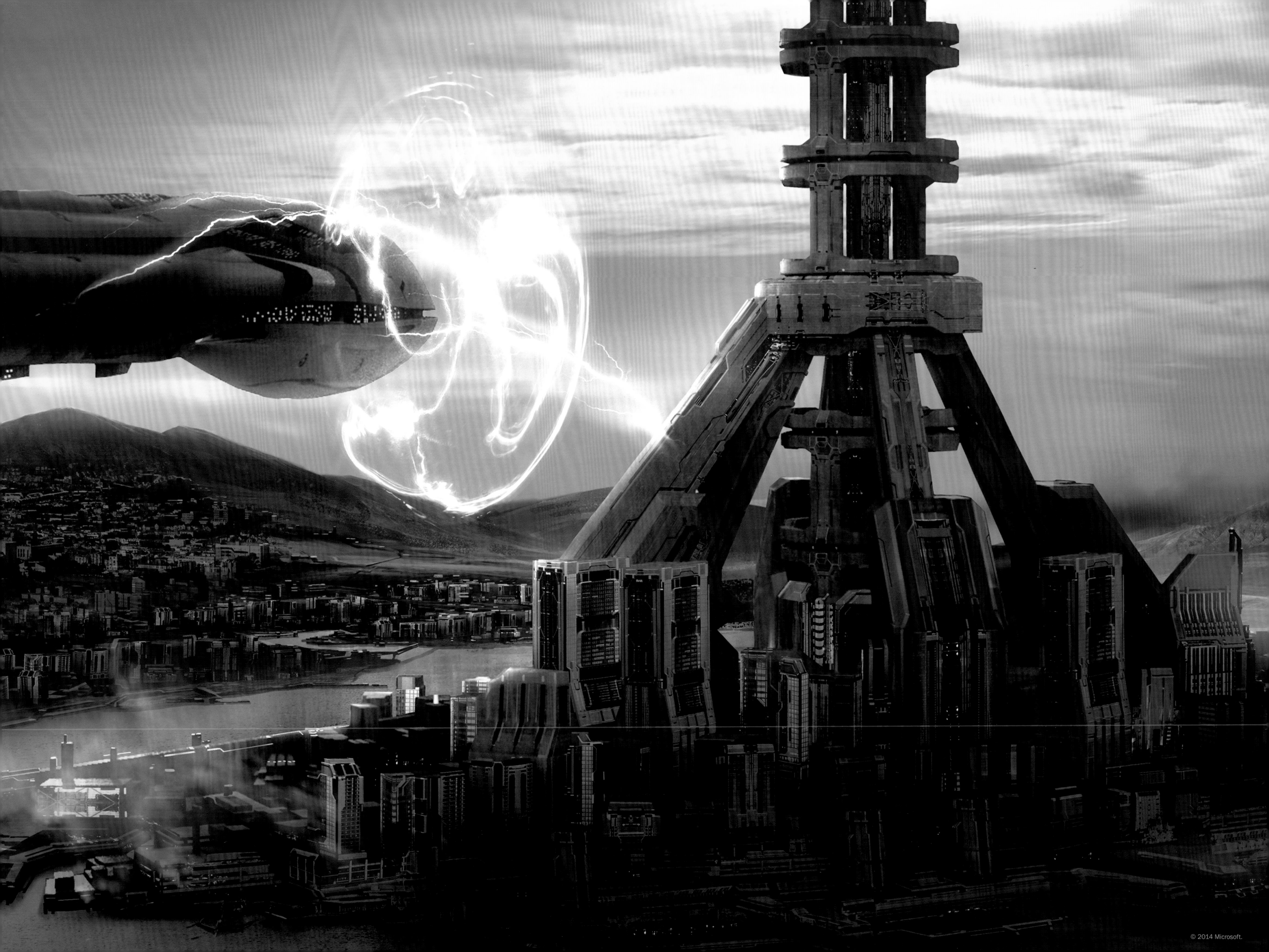

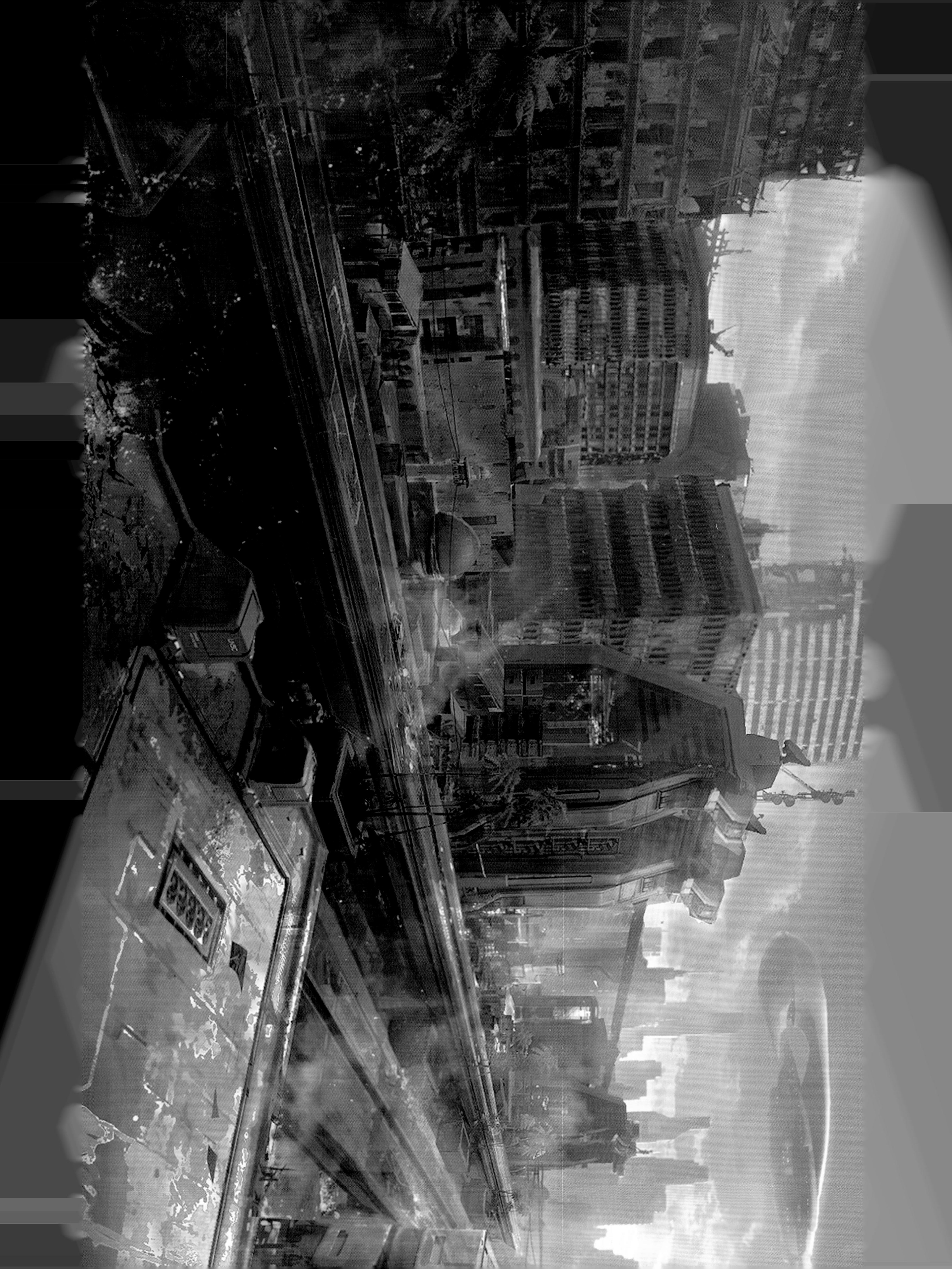

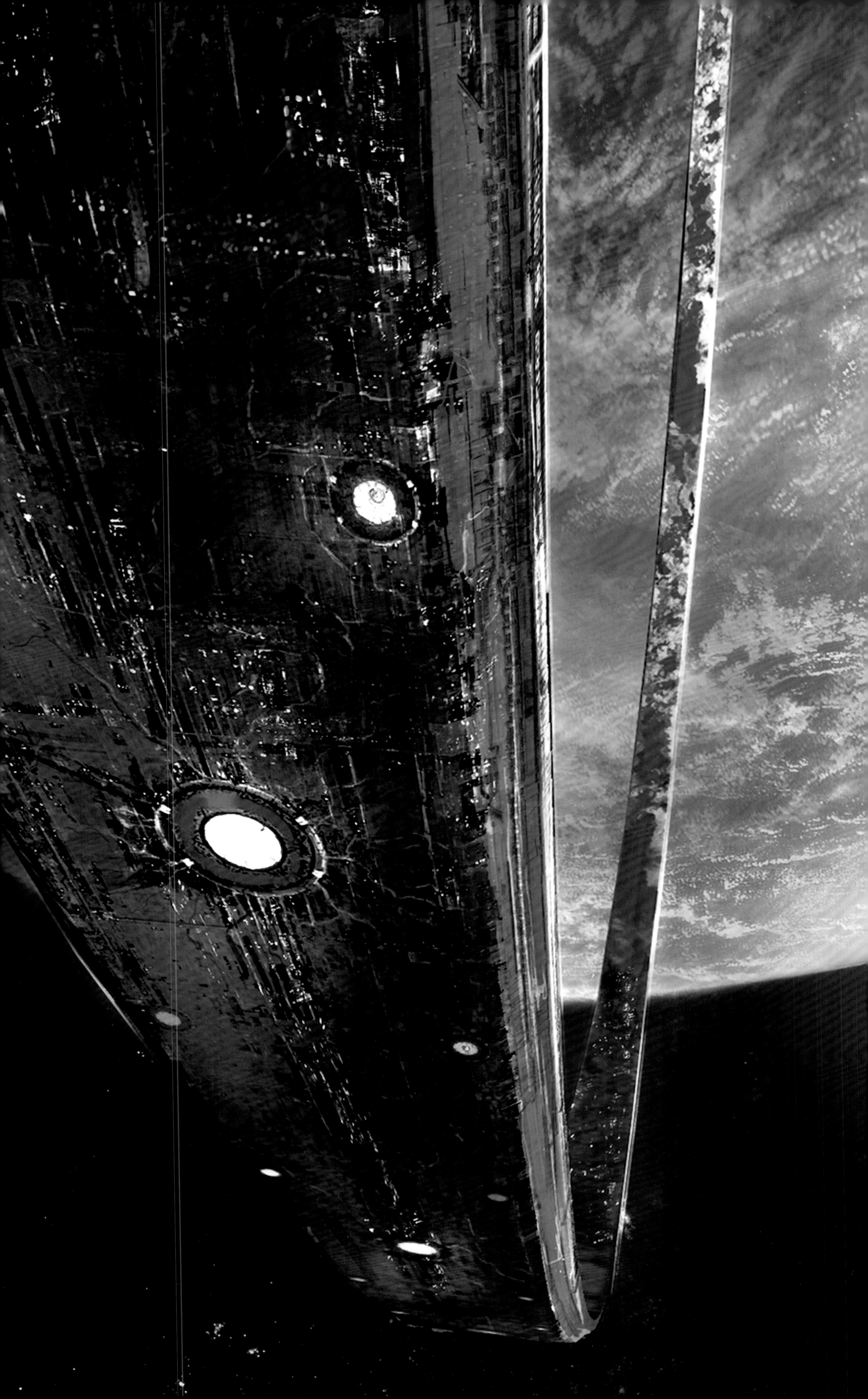

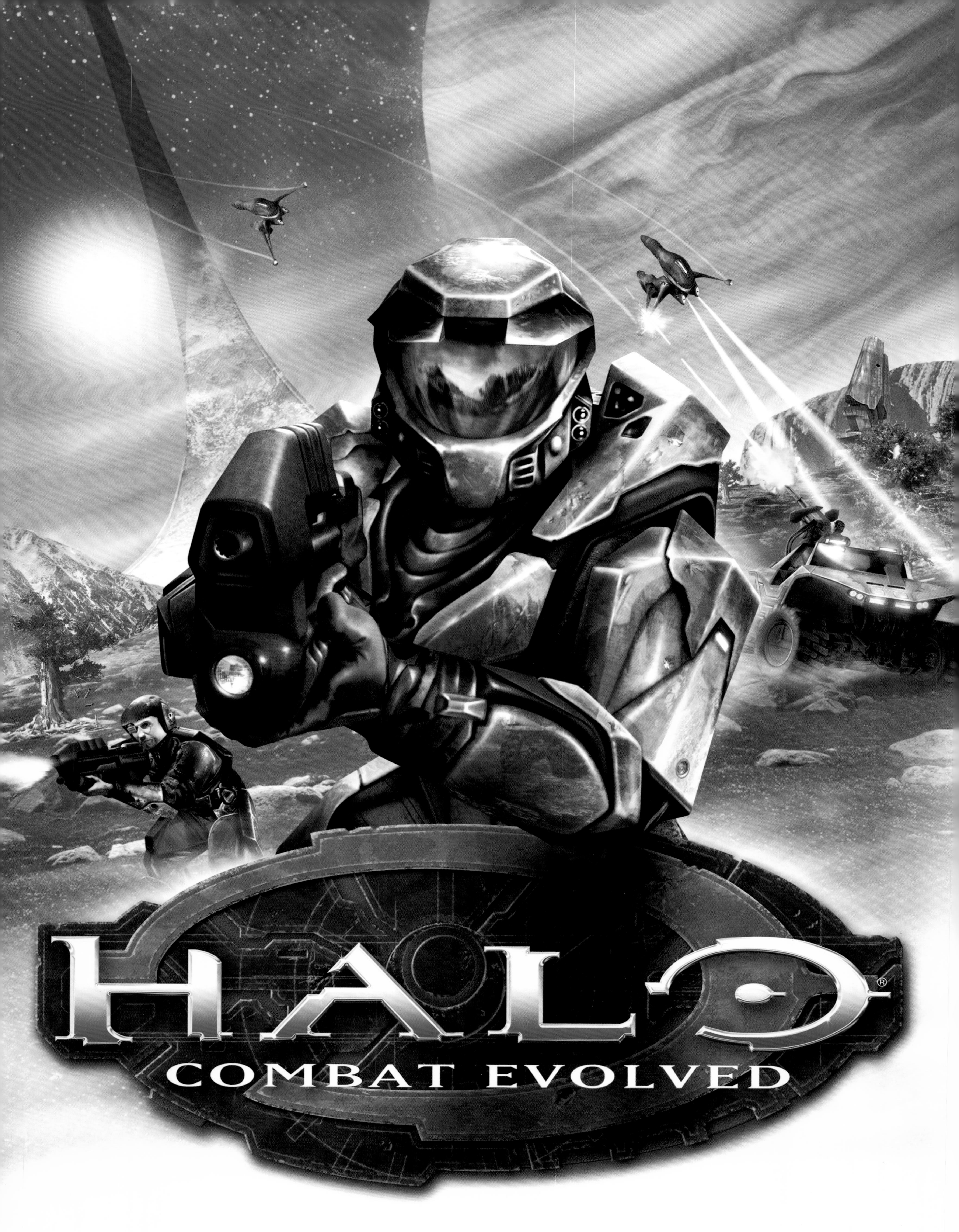
HALO®
COMBAT EVOLVED

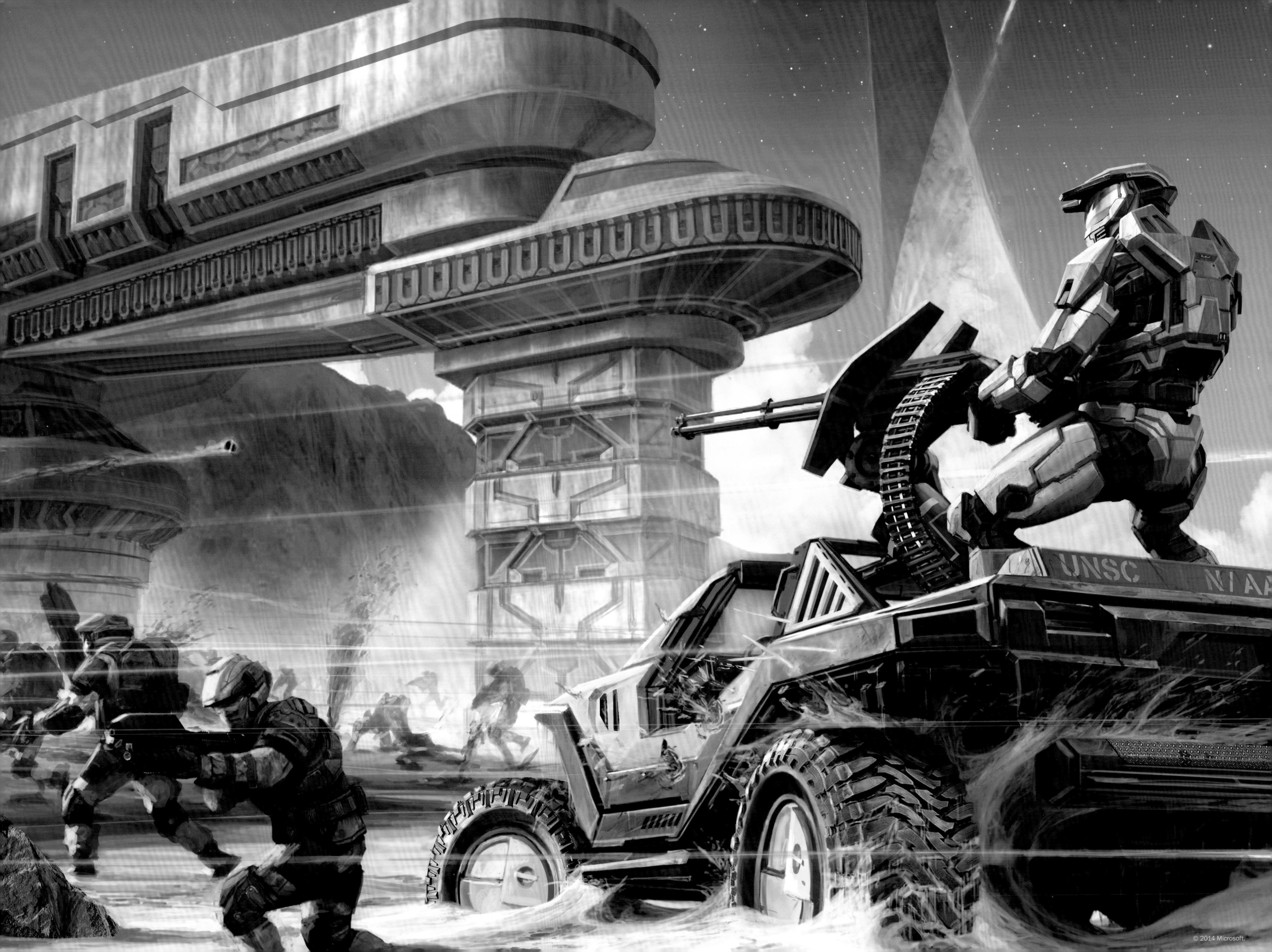
UNSC

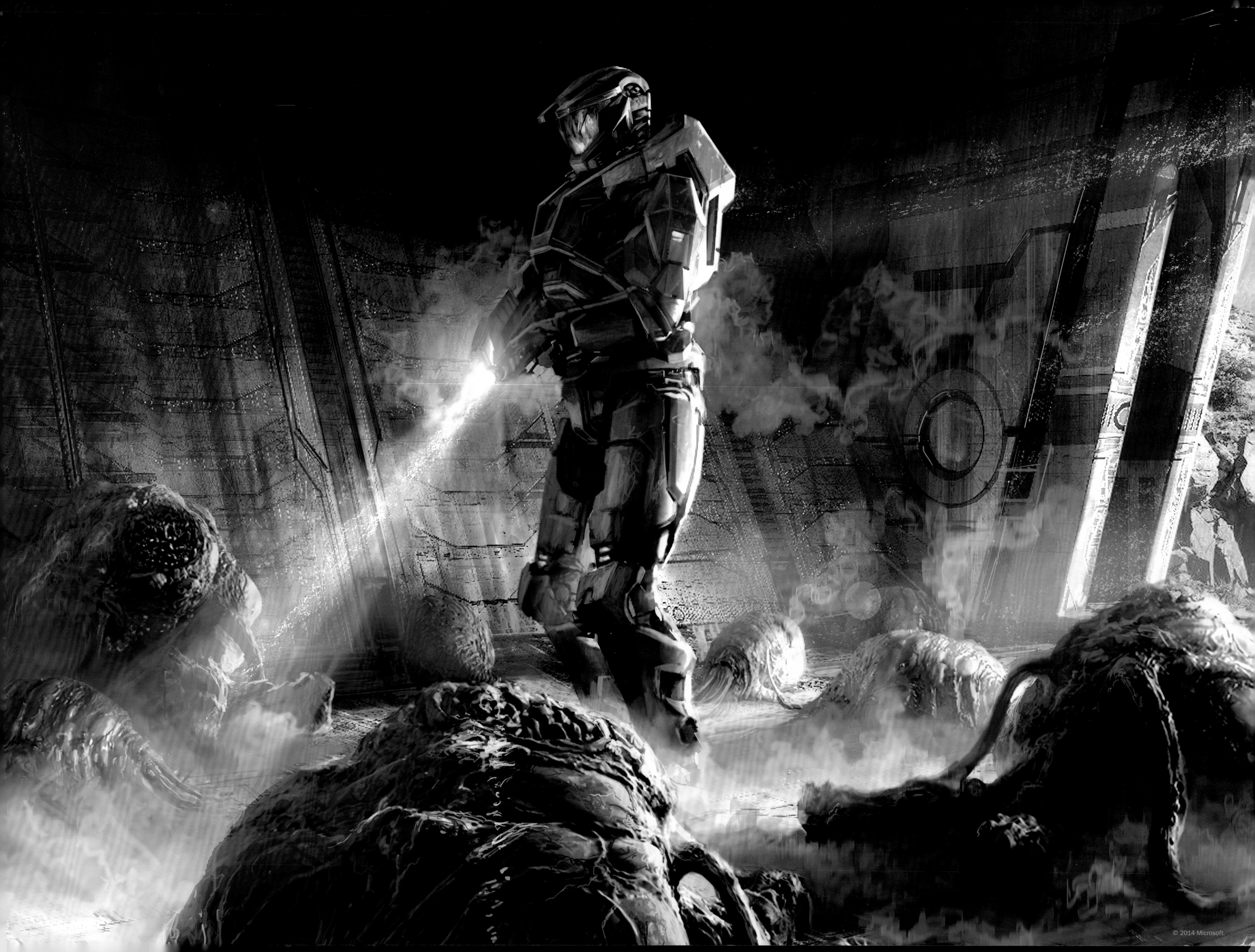

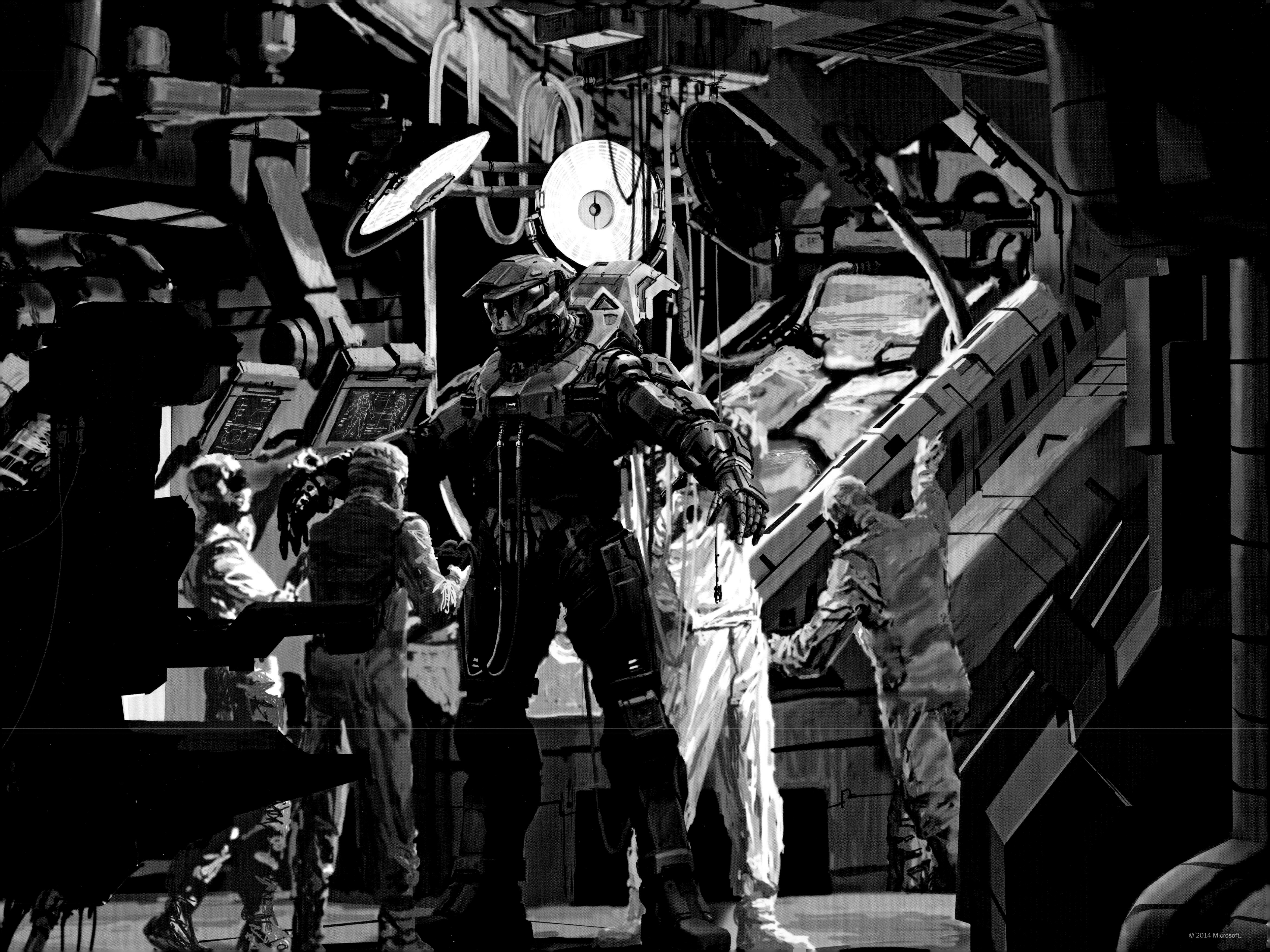

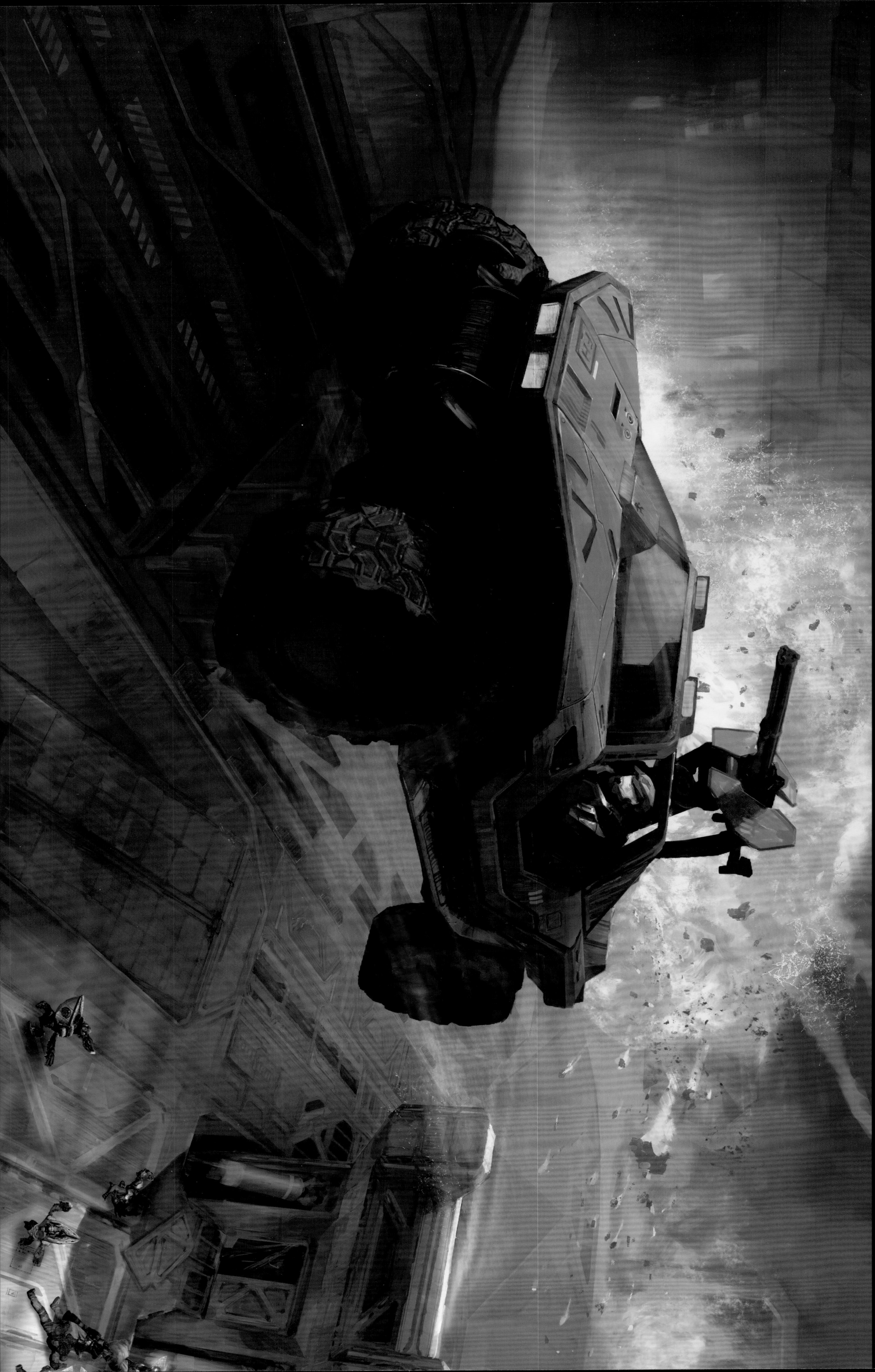

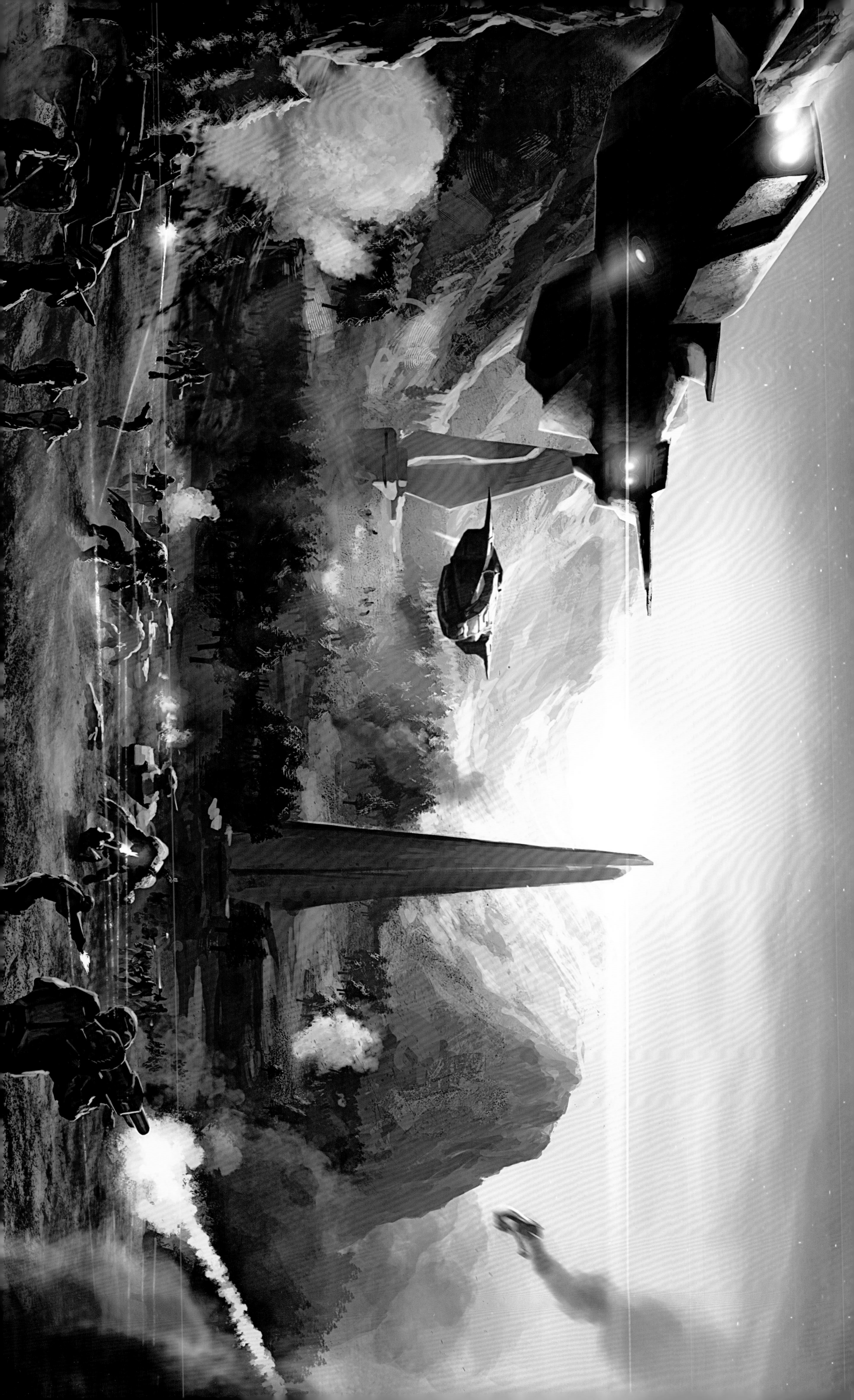

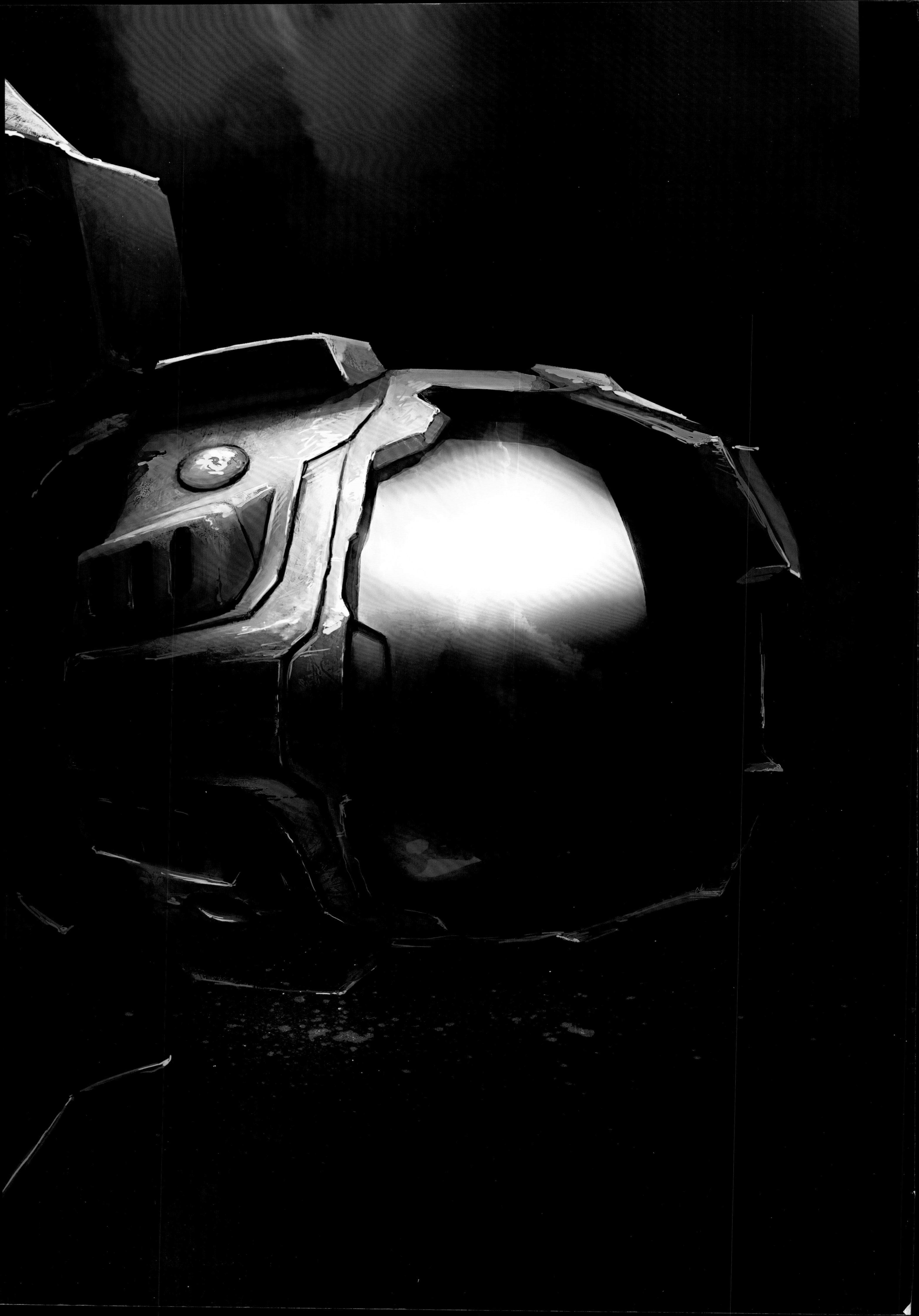

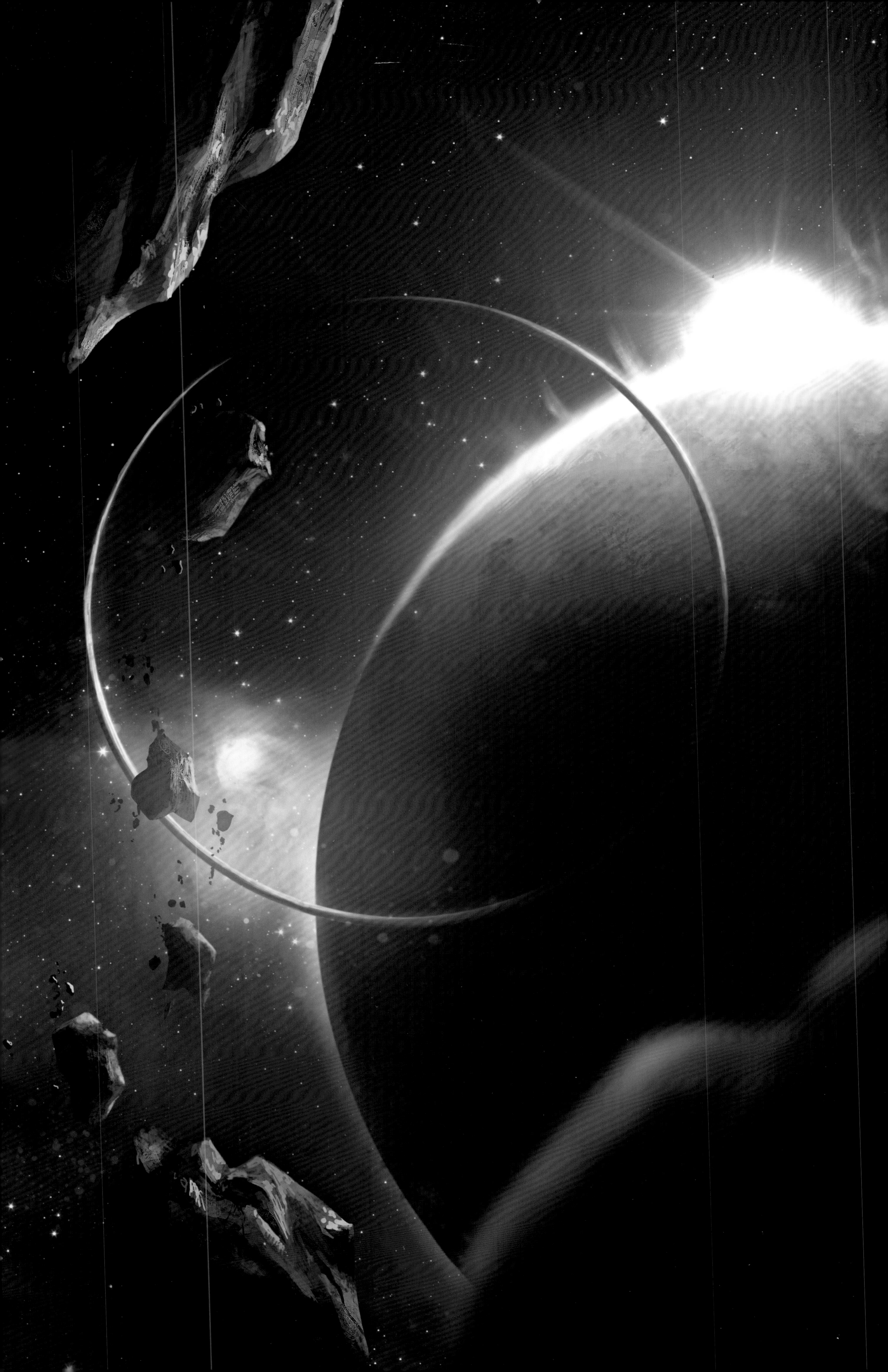

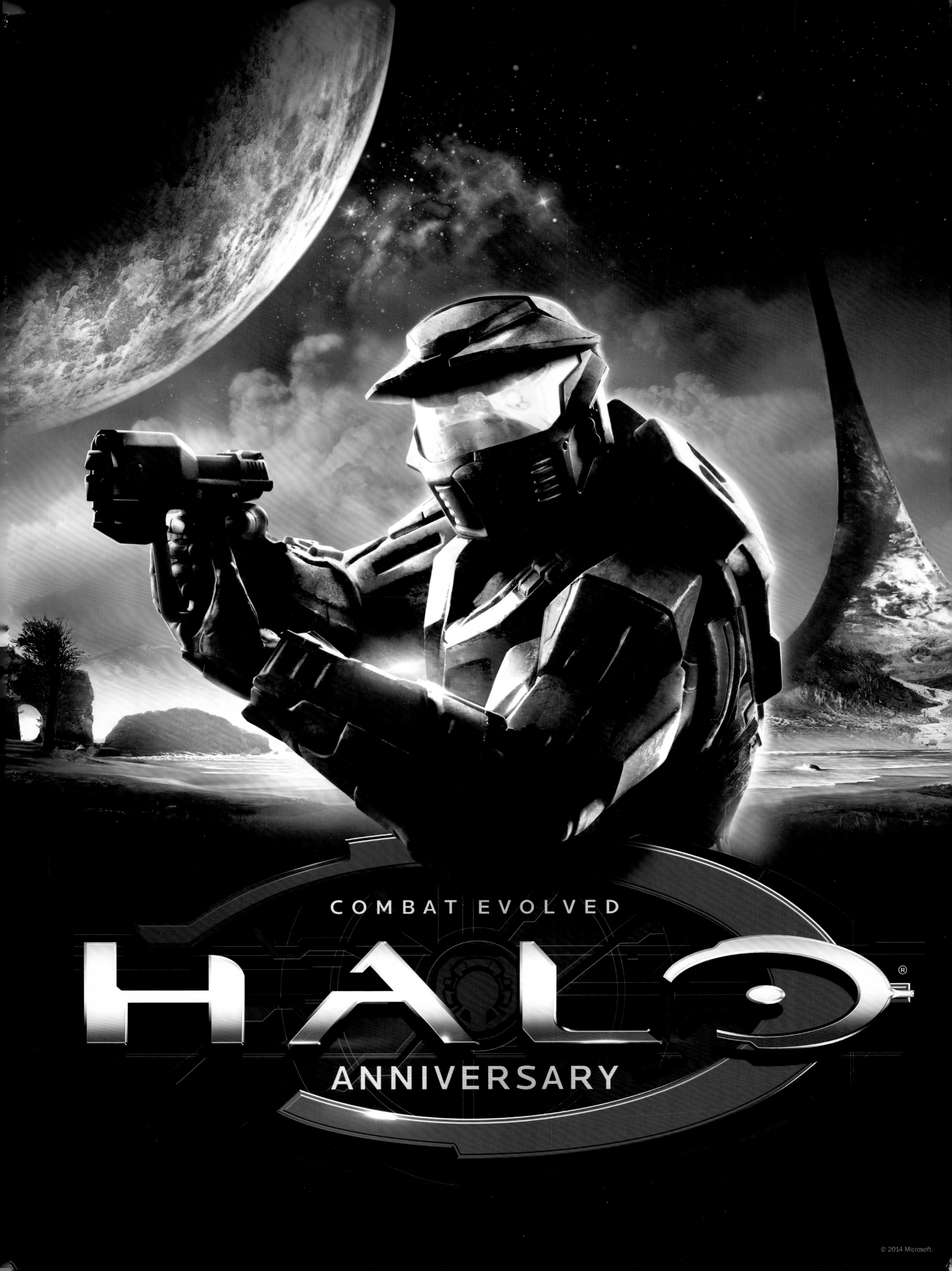
COMBAT EVOLVED
HALO®
ANNIVERSARY